THE WILD DUCK

THE WILD DUCK

after Ibsen

a new adaptation by Robert Icke

OBERON BOOKS
LONDON

WWW.OBERONBOOKS.COM

First published in 2018 by Oberon Books Ltd
521 Caledonian Road, London N7 9RH
Tel: +44 (0) 20 7607 3637 / Fax: +44 (0) 20 7607 3629
e-mail: info@oberonbooks.com
www.oberonbooks.com

A catalogue record for this book is available from the British Library.

PB ISBN: 9781786826589
E ISBN: 9781786826572

Cover design by James Illman

Printed and bound by 4EDGE Limited, Hockley, Essex, UK.
eBook conversion by CPI Group (UK) Ltd, Croydon, CR0 4YY.

Visit www.oberonbooks.com to read more about all our books and to buy them. You will also find features, author interviews and news of any author events, and you can sign up for e-newsletters so that you're always first to hear about our new releases.

Printed on FSC accredited paper

I can take any empty space and call it a bare stage. A man walks across this empty space whilst someone else is watching him, and this is all that is needed for an act of theatre to be engaged.

Peter Brook, *The Empty Space*

Each partner strives to find in the other, or induces the other to become, the very embodiment of the other whose co-operation is required as a complement of the particular identity he feels compelled to sustain.

R.D. Laing, *The Self and Others*

Acknowledgements

My greatest debt is to the actors and creative team of the original production, whose ideas, instincts and input quite literally make the show, and to all of whom I am genuinely grateful.

This sort of work would scarcely be possible without the support and backing of its originating theatre – on multiple levels, I'm thankful to my whole team at the Almeida, who, five years in, are really my Almeida family – and on this one, as on so many before, I owe big thanks to Rupert Goold, Lucy Pattison, Denise Wood, Emma Pritchard, Rebecca Frecknall and Stephanie Bain.

And on top of that, thanks to everyone else who read the play or watched a performance and gave suggestions or support – significantly: Rachel Taylor, Helena Clark, Stephen Grosz, David Hare, Helen Lewis, Josh Higgott, Jon Sedmak, Laura Marling, Andrew Scott, Ben Naylor, Ilinca Radulian, Denzel Wesley-Sanderson and Zara Tempest-Walters.

RI, October 2018

This adaptation was commissed by and originally produced at the Almeida, where it had its first performance on 15th October, 2018.

Cast (in alphabetical order)

Charles Woods	Nicholas Day
Hedwig Ekdal	Grace Doherty
Francis Ekdal	Nicholas Farrell
Anna Sowerby	Andrea Hall
Gregory Woods	Kevin Harvey
James Ekdal	Edward Hogg
Gina Ekdal	Lyndsey Marshal
Hedwig Ekdal	Clara Read
John Relling	Rick Warden

Creative Team

Direction	Robert Icke
Design	Bunny Christie
Light	Elliot Griggs
Sound	Tom Gibbons
Casting	Julia Horan CDG
Costume Supervision	Claire Wardroper
Fight Direction	Kevin McCurdy
Assistant Direction	Denzel Westley-Sanderson
Design Assistant	Verity Sadler
Photography	Manuel Harlan
Company Stage Manager	Claire Sibley
Deputy Stage Manager	Adam Cox
Assistant Stage Manager	Beth Cotton

[ACT ONE]

Bare stage. Emptiness.

As the evening progresses, the stage will move, piece by piece, towards a kind of naturalism – a subtle and unobtrusive progression towards the final image of the Ekdals' home. Think of it like a photograph developing. The actors start in what feel like rehearsal clothes, and move slowly – item by item – into costume.

The lights are bright. As the evening progresses they will get darker and darker.

The actor playing GREGORY comes out and waits for the audience to fall silent. When they do, he switches on a handheld microphone (or just speaks to them directly if you prefer: the aim is the difference between this mode of speech and normal dialogue). When characters are speaking into a mic, their name is followed by (m) – and they are speaking to the audience. Ideally, the microphones seem objective, like 'the truth'. To start with at least.

GREGORY (m)   The devices – this is just a reminder [to turn them off]. Even if you think you've already done it, that feeling certain – that feeling could be wrong. We don't need intrusions; the world can wait for a few hours. Anyway, it's all lies.

The play has started.

Hello.

In 1884, Henrik Ibsen wrote *The Wild Duck*. People say they want to see the real version, true to Ibsen, but that version is in Norwegian – actually, a sort of out-dated Danish-Norwegian, so even if we could do it, you very likely wouldn't understand it. We would say words you couldn't understand and ones we can't mean. And saying things you don't mean – well, there's a word for that, and it's 'lying'. I mean, to tell the

1

story like that would be a sort of lie. Going through the motions. The real thing buried somewhere underneath.

In the beginning one person would have stood before you and told the story. Told the truth, I suppose – it's funny, we *tell* the truth, don't we, we don't say it, we *tell* it, it's a tale, it has to be – carefully packaged.

And then – we started to pretend. Tell you we aren't who we are and the stage is a sky or a battlefield or a funfair. We started to lie. And the illusion bit in, the edges blurred and you forgot about truths and instead you only wanted to make your time go by, take a break from thinking about how disappointing everything is these days, how it's all lies. But even if you heap lies on top of truth, it waits underneath.

So this is a true story

In 1884, Henrik Ibsen wrote *The Wild Duck*. He was a white man. He was fifty-six years old. He was Norwegian. He had a strict routine that he stuck to until he died. He's dead now. As a much younger man, he had fathered an illegitimate child on a young girl. When he was a child, his father was declared bankrupt. He had a sister called Hedvig. There are more facts, but we'd be here all night, and anyway, probably none of them are relevant –

Anyway. My character, Gregory Woods, on his first day home – where he was brought up, I mean, not [home] – he's decided to come back. It's the first time he's been back for several years. And, as the afternoon is deep and the light is starting to turn creamy, he pauses outside a familiar house, an imposing, detached townhouse, buttons his top button, puts on a white bow tie, slides the familiar, heavy gate aside, and in his jet-black shoes, crunches his way up the drive –

This story starts in the entrance hall of a dinner party.

JAMES Gregers? My god, you look exactly the same –

JAMES takes the microphone from GREGORY

JAMES (m) This is a lie.

GREGORY And you look *incredible* –

(m) James Ekdal and Gregory Woods – my character – were friends at school but now, this evening is the first time they have set eyes on each other for over fifteen years.

JAMES addresses a member of the audience.

JAMES (m) I'm sorry to bother you, but I couldn't just borrow your jacket, could I? I won't damage it, you'll get it back – they're insured here (I hope). Thank you.

JAMES borrows a coat or a jacket from the audience.

Imagine this jacket is a deep, bottle green. It's clean, it's well-made, but its appearance this evening, right now, worn by my character, James Ekdal, seems – *eccentric*.

The invitation said 'white tie'. James had thought that white tie meant any suit worn with a white tie. His father had – his father had told him – sorry – he'd borrowed his father's dress suit. As the other guests arrived in black suits, white shirts – in white tie – James could only see one colour. Green.

3

GREGORY   You really do look incredible.

Is there something homoerotic about GREGORY's gaze on JAMES?
Maybe.

JAMES   Don't. I'm embarrassed, actually – I hadn't
             realised

He gestures around him.

GREGORY   What?

JAMES   This place: it's like a royal palace.

GREGORY   But you've been here before?

JAMES   No – [why would I have been?]

GREGORY   But – *sorry* –

             given the – your relationship with my father –

JAMES   Are you sure he invited me tonight?

GREGORY   [Yes] – You're on the seating plan – but –
             hang on

             Sorry

             I've not *spoken* to him much, or at all, really,
             but he *writes* to me, usually when there's
             something with the company, but he implied
             he'd been supporting you –

JAMES   Oh, he *has*, he absolutely has, he's been so
             generous – since, what happened to my
             father – you know [about that]

GREGORY   *(Quickly.)* Yes – of course

                          ,

JAMES (m)   Francis Ekdal – my father – had been
             a partner in Woods and Son and it was
             his signature on the company's financial
             accounts when around the world, the

4

bubbles burst and the markets sank. And to tell you the briefest version of the story, it turned out that key investments hadn't been registered – and so didn't officially exist. The company's stock dropped two thirds of its value. People lost their savings. And Francis Ekdal was tried, found guilty, served with a fine he would never live long enough to pay, and a ten-year, minimum security prison term for investment fraud.

GREGORY   How is he, your dad? Do you see much of him?

JAMES   Lives with us, now. And he's all right. He's – all right.

(m)   He's never been the same.

But let's not talk about him, anyway, it's – it's not, the [best topic of conversation]

How are *you*? Where have you been all this time?

GREGORY   Oh, you know, here and there. Seeking higher ground. Thinking, mainly.

JAMES   And you've been happy?

GREGORY   Lonely. I've been lonely. You know, I thought I saw him before – your father –

JAMES   Here? No.

GREGORY   I'm *sure* it was

JAMES   No, it must have been someone else, it couldn't have been him

GREGORY   We should go in.

JAMES a bit jumpy, suddenly –

JAMES   Go in?

5

GREGORY   For dinner? I know it's early but for some
                 reason they want to eat while it's light –

JAMES   Yes. You know, actually I had a list of names.
                 Of the guests. To have them fresh in the mind.
                 There's only twelve, well, you and your father
                 are both Woods, and then me, so there's only
                 nine, but I've gone and left it in the bathroom,
                 I'll just be a minute – back in one minute –

JAMES exits.

*As GREGORY picks up the mic to talk to the audience – enter
FRANCIS. He's an elderly man, kindly but absent. He might be
drunk. He behaves as if he's interrupted the scene – as if the actor
has come out at the wrong moment. Terrified by the presence of the
audience, he looks straight at them.*

FRANCIS   I'm sorry –

                 ,

                 you've started, haven't you?

GREGORY is horrified – open-mouthed – to see FRANCIS.

GREGORY   The party? Yes – they've just gone in for
                 dinner –

FRANCIS   I had the wrong sheets. I had the wrong
                 pages. I pick them up here – it's easier – but
                 I wanted to get them before it started and get
                 back home. I really didn't want to be here
                 when all the people were here.

GREGORY is shocked to see FRANCIS like this.

GREGORY   Francis? Don't worry – I want to help you

FRANCIS   No, my friend, but thank you –

GREGORY   I'm Gregory. Charles' son.

                 You don't remember me.

6

FRANCIS looks at GREGORY. Nothing.

FRANCIS   I don't at all.

,

GREGORY   Never mind.

FRANCIS   Never mind, never mind –

JAMES comes back on – sees FRANCIS, suddenly there's a scene –

JAMES   No no *NO* – what the fuck are you doing here? We *had* this conversation. Can you just *go home* – it's *humiliating* –

FRANCIS   Yes – ah – very sorry –

FRANCIS heads for the exit.

GREGORY   He can stay for / dinner if you like –

FRANCIS   No – can't be seen to / do that

JAMES   Can YOU JUST GO HOME –

FRANCIS has gone.   Oedipal shane

                    Sorry.

GREGORY   I knew it was him.

JAMES   Can we just take a breather out here for a minute before we go in?

,

                    I hate seeing him like this.

                    You don't mind if I smoke, do you?

GREGORY   I'm not sure you can in here – and anyway, it's bad for you –

JAMES   Well, they *say* that –

GREGORY	You're upset.
JAMES	Am I?
	Not with you. With you, honestly, I'm just relieved there's no hard feelings –
GREGORY	Hard feelings? About what?
JAMES	No, I totally understand – when what happened happened, I had to stand up for my dad, and you had to stand up for yours –
GREGORY	But why would I hold that against you?
JAMES	It's okay – he *told* me not to contact you: I wanted to write and apologise – for what dad had done, to try and make amends, but Mr Woods – I mean, your dad said there would be no point-– which I understood.
GREGORY	Ah.
	He may have been right.
	I'm still [surprised] – you've never been here before. So does he come to your place?
JAMES	No. You're very interested (!) in [all of this] – no – Anna does sometimes. His [what's the word?] *friend*. She's a good woman, I think.
GREGORY	So he supports you but – there's a distance –
JAMES	There's a mutual respect, I think. I go to the office. You know, let him know how the business is coming along.
GREGORY	Photography, right?
JAMES	Exactly. Specialists in photographic film.
GREGORY	Film?

JAMES	Your dad said it: find a unique angle. Everyone's carrying a camera these days – but they do digital, and we do film. The dying part of the living art. I mean, we do digital as well –
GREGORY	I didn't even realise you could – that you were a photographer –
JAMES	Well, I wasn't –
GREGORY	I thought you were going to study / at least, my [memory was...]
JAMES	I dropped out – when everything happened, I dropped out to have time to work on Dad's case, but there was never any way we were going to stand against the tide, all the lawyers, the press and everything, totally foregone conclusion – *anyway*. We know what the outcome of that was. And I wasn't in a good way.
GREGORY	But my dad helped you set up – your business –
JAMES	Yes. He's our principal investor. Of course, we'll pay him back, as soon as we get it to the next level, but he's – well, we couldn't have done it without him.
GREGORY	Who's we?
JAMES	Oh – god – yes, I'm married now – of course [you wouldn't know that] – and actually, your father sorted that out too! Gave us a gift of some money which allowed us to actually do it. Our fairy godfather.
GREGORY	Wow.
	But why?
	Sorry – why would he do that?

JAMES	He'd only buried your mother the year before. So I think he understood what it was to be – wounded. We really do respect each other, him and me. And he knew Gina, of course, so he was doubly invested. I wanted you to be there, to be part of the wedding, I mean, but the case, and – well, he said / you were [out of contact] –
GREGORY	Gina –
JAMES	My wife –

JAMES enjoys GREGORY remembering this – waits for him to figure it out –

GREGORY	Gina. The same Gina who worked here – when my mum was ill?
JAMES	Exactly the same Gina.
GREGORY	That's – amazing
JAMES	He's been generous, above and beyond the call of duty. He didn't forget the son of his old friend, when he knew our family was on the ropes.
GREGORY	I didn't think he had it in him.

GREGORY is almost disturbed by this view of his father. In his head, something's not right about it but he can't put his finger on what.

JAMES (m)	And then the sound of a dinner gong.
GREGORY	Well, given everything you've been through, you really do look wonderful –
JAMES	Do I? Thank god you can't see inside. But we keep going – and I have my eye on the future.

Then with a different kind of intimacy –

> Sometimes when I'm lying awake in the
> morning, staring up at the beams, I see them
> pushing his head down to take him out of the
> court. Pushing him down. But not forever.

GREGORY (m) And scene –

The scene ends.

> Gregory Woods had been in the house for
> thirty minutes, and had had exactly one
> conversation – but everything was spinning.
> He put his head against the wall and tried to
> breathe.

JAMES (m) Until the end of it, James Ekdal had barely
noticed that the conversation was happening.
He felt *out of place.* He felt unwelcome, he felt
scared of being exposed – a feeling that's got
its roots deep in class or wealth – and when
you feel like that, it gets harder to focus, hard
to see – because of the bell ringing behind
your eyes.

GREGORY (m) As course after course passed through,
Gregory had the thought that the people
at the table weren't enjoying themselves,
but going through the motions of enjoying
themselves. Their laughter flashed and faded
quickly; their compliments fell flat.

> We go through the motions, don't we?
> We like being rocked because it simulates
> how we were in the womb. We're *not* in
> the womb. But it feels like it. That's how
> it works, we go through the motions, we
> pretend in our own lives, we spin around
> our memories, repeating and repeating our
> traumas. It's not real. Until one day we stop
> – we break the pattern.

JAMES (m)   Later – in the library, after dessert, a very
large man with a very loud voice was trying
to persuade James to do his party trick,
'recite a poem' or 'why don't you take our
photograph?' He was smiling, but James felt
small.

GREGORY (m)   Charles Woods, the father of Gregory
Woods, laid out some rare bottles of wine on
the table, dusty from the cellar, and looked
straight at James. 1885, he said, or '89? The
room fell quiet.

JAMES   Let's have the third one – the '89. Let's go
strong. I've never actually had, uh, chamber
tin –

And suddenly CHARLES WOODS is there, and we're into a scene:

CHARLES   *Chambertin.*

JAMES   I'm sorry?

CHARLES   The wine. Chamber tin. *Chambertin.* It's
French.

JAMES   Sorry, yes, chamber tin – of course – well,
the strongest of the three Chambertin-s it is.
18, 85 or 89, you said – so '89. Go for the
top. I think. No?

A pause. Another faux pas. CHARLES isn't cruel here.

CHARLES   1889. They're vintages, those numbers:
1889 is the year the grapes were grown and
harvested. The taste is really the difference in
time between the day it was bottled and now;
so the moment you choose to drink it – to
uncork it and let it meet the air – is *everything*

JAMES (m)   And scene –

A few minutes later, James excused himself and went to the bathroom and vomited. After the bathroom, he let himself out and walked the three miles home. Nobody noticed that he'd gone.

GREGORY (m)   The stories we tell tell us. Who we are. And old stories tell us truths about where we came from. And – how we can change.

Gregory Woods stared at his father. He seemed older, his face was harder – like a leather map of cruelties past. The guests had started to leave, the staff were clearing glasses and closing curtains

The scene clicks into beginning.

CHARLES   Gregory, I wish you hadn't insisted on having the Ekdal boy here tonight.

GREGORY   Why not?

CHARLES   Can't you count? Thirteen at the table.

GREGORY   So you don't believe in morals but you do believe in *that*. And Francis Ekdal, your colleague, your best man, wandering around half-destitute and half demented – *you* were his friend –

CHARLES   Yes. And I've paid the price for that friendship.

GREGORY   Your reputation took a knock: he went to prison.

CHARLES   Oh god – it went to trial. The evidence was clear, and so was the verdict.

GREGORY   That's the story, that's the illusion –

CHARLES   An acquittal means not guilty.

GREGORY   People in the street spat at him. He lost
                 everything. He lost who he was. And who
                 benefitted from that? The person who now
                 had a majority share – *convenient*, that,
                 somehow –

CHARLES   Gregory, you were *there*, then, you saw all
                 the papers before / it went to court

GREGORY   Mum was ill. I couldn't think – I couldn't *see*
                 that you were already spinning your webs –

CHARLES   I'm not sure how you think I could have
                 influenced anything, if / that's –

GREGORY   The usual way. Your sort code and your
                 account number.

CHARLES   I don't know why you're being so abrupt –

GREGORY   I am being *honest*. For the first time, perhaps.
                 Honest.

CHARLES   Right. Are we done?

GREGORY (m)   It took a lot for Gregory Woods to resist his
                 father. He'd known a confrontation would
                 come, but now, here, he could only see how
                 imposing Charles was – how he felt like a
                 man who was *right*.

                 You don't feel guilty, then?

CHARLES   When Francis Ekdal came out of prison, he was
                 a broken man. I've arranged some work for him,
                 I pay him a blasted sight more than it's worth,
                 and, while trying to safeguard the reputation
                 of the company, I do my bit for him –

GREGORY *(sarc)* Right –

CHARLES   It isn't cheap, you know?

GREGORY   And how much is setting up a photography
                 studio?

CHARLES	I'm sorry?
GREGORY	How much did it cost to set up their business?
CHARLES	I don't understand why something I did out of kindness is interrogated as if it's a *crime*
GREGORY	Because it isn't kindness. Not really. It never is with you.
CHARLES	Okay. Everything's so simple, isn't it?
GREGORY	No. But some things are.
CHARLES	You've been happy enough to take my money. The company's money. You could have set something up on your own –
GREGORY	And what space is there left, Dad, what space did you leave for young people to come along and do something different, do something for themselves, without being son of Charles Woods, the 'son' of 'Woods & Son' – but let's keep on the scent – more than a decade ago, you wrote to me, on your headed paper, short letter, as usual, needing me to return some documents, my shareholding or something, I can't remember, but what I *do* remember is the casual, casual postscript: that 'the Ekdal son' was getting married.
CHARLES	I was trying to make a connection with you –
GREGORY	What you didn't see fit to mention was that he was marrying someone who worked for us, in this house, when Mum was alive –

,

CHARLES   Gina had long since left by then – and I
           didn't think she was your type, Greg, I didn't
           know you'd taken such an interest –

GREGORY   I hadn't. But someone had.

CHARLES   I don't follow –

GREGORY   *You.*

CHARLES   I'm not sure which particular rumours you're
           / focussing on

GREGORY   Dad. You can stop the lies because *my mother
           told me* before she passed away. Told me
           everything.

           ,

           You want to know why I went, you can think
           about / that –

CHARLES   And you're happy to accept her view of
           things? Her view of me?

GREGORY   Yes. Because she told me the trauma she
           suffered –

CHARLES   I'm sorry to burst your bubble but she didn't
           suffer – at least, no more than could be
           helped with her condition. And I can tell
           you, she had the very best available / care

GREGORY   Sort code. Account number. Same reason
           you married her.

CHARLES   And if you really wanted to talk to me about
           this, you could have done it *then,* rather
           than run for the hills when her body was
           still warm in the grave – and then file your
           complaint sixteen years later.

GREGORY   I didn't run for the hills – my mother died –

CHARLES	Greg, I don't want to argue. You up and vanish, not so much as a birthday card most years, and then, when the prodigal son returns, you want to dig up fights that finished years ago. Well I don't.
GREGORY	You in*sisted* I come back –
CHARLES	Well, you could have said no –
GREGORY	I thought you might be ill –
CHARLES	I am ill –

GREGORY doesn't believe this –

GREGORY	Are you? What do you really want? Why am I here?
CHARLES	You're here because I wanted to say to you that, if you were willing, I would hand over the company to you. It's already got your name on it.
GREGORY	Why would I take on something corrupt?
CHARLES	To remake it. To make it better. I can't do it in the same way anymore – it's time for new energy. I'm too old and my eyes are getting weak –
GREGORY	They always were weak
	,
CHARLES	I know there's a lot of – mess – between us. History. I do know that. But I'm your father and I do / love you
GREGORY	What do you *want?*
CHARLES	I'm old, Gregory. I'm lonely – have been all my life. It'd be nice to have you around and involved. Nice to have a conversation. Nice to hand my son the thing I've spent my life creating.

GREGORY   You've got Anna.

CHARLES   I have. She's a wonder, quite frankly.

GREGORY   Then strap her down. Marry her.

CHARLES lowers his head. GREGORY has hit on the truth.

CHARLES   Would you be opposed to that?

GREGORY   Why would I care?

CHARLES   Because since we buried your mother /
               there's

GREGORY   I'm not a romantic.

CHARLES   Well. Thank you, whatever you are.

*A penny drops in GREGORY's mind. And it makes him angry, angry
enough to set events in motion –*

GREGORY   And that's it. That's why I'm here, isn't it?
               That's why the party. The estranged son
               returns, forgives the father, implicitly blesses
               the wedding – which is already planned? Of
               course it is. This was just a – *photo opportunity.*
               Happy families. And all those stories about
               Charles Woods – the ones about how the
               vicious bully hammered his first wife into her
               grave – well, they can't be true if the son's
               come back and giving it all his blessing.

CHARLES   God, the way you hate me –

GREGORY   I'm the only one who sees you.

CHARLES   But with your mother's eyes – and she didn't
               see things clearly.

GREGORY   So she made up the other women, did she?
               That was her fault, that you went whirling off
               with whoever caught your eye, big grin on
               your face – and then writing a cheque for the
               consequences –

CHARLES	Word for word. It's like hearing her speak.
GREGORY	So what my mother told me was a lie?
CHARLES	I don't need to be spoken to like this –
GREGORY	God, what you've *done* to people, Dad – [I don't know] how you sleep! So many lives you've shattered and pushed under the carpet – like chicken bones under your feet – and you think the whole thing's buried so far down that nothing can ever come back –
CHARLES	I don't know how to talk to you, Gregory –
GREGORY	I agree. You don't.

'

CHARLES	I do have regrets. I do.
	But I think, if you're in my house, to treat me with respect / is hardly
GREGORY	I was thinking the same thing: I'm going to go.
CHARLES	Go?
GREGORY	Leave.
CHARLES	It's getting dark, Greg – you don't have to leave.
GREGORY	And yet – I'm leaving.
CHARLES	Don't end up lonely, Gregory.
GREGORY (m)	And *scene* –
	Seeing the truth can be a gradual process. But then there's the moment. The moment when you really *hear,* really understand, the lyrics of an old song; the moment when your eyes adjust to the darkness, or an old story

suddenly exposes its real meaning. When the floor of an old system gives way. In 1884, Henrik Ibsen wrote *The Wild Duck*.

[ACT TWO]

… but in fact, there are no breaks between the acts, they're just here to help organise rehearsals.

HEDWIG enters. She's twelve but she seems younger. GINA enters, starts to prepare. A black curtain starts to descend, lowering the height of the stage picture. GREGORY explains to us:

The top floor of a nineteenth-century house, converted into flats by someone long forgotten. It's three miles away from the house of Charles Woods, in one of those areas where people with aspirations pretend it's in a different, nearby, area when actually – it's in this one.

It isn't a palace, but it is a home. The ceiling hangs low. A bulb dangles from the roof, where once-white paint is cracking and stained – a wooden floor, an old sofa, a battered brown armchair, a record player, a work table – that have all seen better days.

GINA (m)

The Ekdals used to own the whole house, but a few years earlier, they sold it. The ground floor flat was privately rented, but they'd kept a lifetime lease on the first and second floors. But times got harder, the money from the sale ran out – and so the Ekdals had recently taken a practical decision – to move their lives up into the second floor, into their photography studio, and rent out their bedroom on the floor below.

Gina Ekdal – my character – is staring at an old calculator and a series of receipts trying to make sense of where all the money went *this week*.

GINA	Heddy.
	Heddy.
	Are you reading?
HEDWIG	No. Yes.
GINA	Come on. Not this late. Do you remember how much we paid for Dad's butter?
HEDWIG	Three pounds twenty-nine.
GINA	Did we? The amount of butter we get through. Is there any left?

HEDWIG opens a butter dish. It's empty.

| HEDWIG | Not much. |
| GINA | And sausages and beer and cheese. That comes to … |

She does the calculation.

	A lot of money.
HEDWIG	But we've saved some by us not having dinner this evening because we weren't hungry.
GINA	That's true. And those photographs sold.
HEDWIG	Yes that really is good isn't it?
GINA	Mmmhmm
	,
HEDWIG	I wonder what Daddy's doing now.
GINA	Mmmhmm
HEDWIG	Talking probably. Or maybe he's eating. No, I think he's talking.
GINA	Mmmhmm

HEDWIG	He'll be talking to Mr Woods.

GINA, not obviously, looks up.

GINA	Maybe

FRANCIS comes in.

	You're late back.
FRANCIS	They'd shut the back door, the buggers, but nevertheless, I got in and picked up another big batch of receipts. At least a week's worth.
GINA	I could just go to the office and pick them up for you –
FRANCIS	No, no, good to get out – Corporal Ekdal, reporting for inspection, lieutenant.
HEDWIG	Very good, corporal – all in order.
FRANCIS	Do I need to patrol the forest, sir?
HEDWIG	Everyone asleep up there, corporal
FRANCIS	Very good, lieutenant. Permission to retire for the night?
HEDWIG	Permission granted. Stand down, corporal.
FRANCIS	Permission to kiss the lieutenant on the head?
HEDWIG	Permission granted.

They salute. As he heads off to bed –

GINA	There's a bottle in your pocket, corporal.

,

FRANCIS	Is there?
	Deal with that problem later, I will, colonel.

There isn't a bottle – at least, not that we can see. Off he goes.

HEDWIG	Does Granddad get paid for his work?
GINA	Yes, he does, but – don't tell your dad.
HEDWIG	What do you think Daddy's doing *now*?
GINA	I don't know, sweetheart –
HEDWIG	Do you think he's eating delicious food? Like a – pie. Or cheese. Or chocolate mousse.
GINA	Maybe he is. Are you hungry?
HEDWIG	No.
GINA	Really?
HEDWIG	No –
	Anyway Daddy promised he'd bring a treat back for me.
GINA	You can still eat something –
HEDWIG	But I don't want to be full because we don't know what the treat *is*. Do you think he'll be in a good mood?
GINA	Maybe. Though I wish someone had asked about the room.
HEDWIG	Mm.
	This is worrying.
	,
	But – he'll be in a good mood tonight anyway because he's had that dinner and because Grandad's happy so that's two things – and even if we had got someone to rent the bedroom it'd be a waste of good news on a night when he'll already be in a good mood so it's better as it is. I think.

FRANCIS comes back in.

GINA   Where's he going?

HEDWIG   Sink.

GINA (m)   When the Ekdals had moved into the photography studio on the top floor they couldn't afford to put in a kitchen. So a small work sink had to suffice – but if you needed the kitchen, or indeed the bathroom, it was a trip down a flight of stairs to the floor they used to live on.

FRANCIS is caught, slightly shamefaced – with a whisky glass.

FRANCIS   Had to get this –

He waves a pair of glasses as he scarpers.

GINA   Where do you think he gets the money from?

HEDWIG   For his drink? Isn't it from his work?

GINA   No, they send that straight to me –

HEDWIG   I dunno. Maybe someone gives him it.

GINA (m)   And scene. This evening wasn't an unusual evening. This is how it was.

Enter JAMES, still in the jacket.

JAMES   Helloo-oo

GINA   You're back early –

HEDWIG   Daddy!

HEDWIG races to her father and greets him.

                How was it? What did you eat? Who was there?

JAMES   Lots of people were there.

HEDWIG   And did you talk to all of them?

JAMES	I did, but Gregers monopolised me, somewhat –
GINA	God, Gregory Woods. Is he still the same?
JAMES	He is indeed still the same
HEDWIG	Who was there? What did you eat?
JAMES	Shoes!

HEDWIG pulls his shoes off for him

	Is the old man not back yet?
HEDWIG	He's in his room –
JAMES	Is he alright?
HEDWIG	He's fine
GINA	Why wouldn't he be?
JAMES	No, there's no [reason] – I'll nip in and see him before he puts his head down
GINA	I wouldn't –
JAMES	Oh he's – D-R-I-N-K-I-N-G?
GINA	He is.
JAMES	Poor old thing – let him have his pleasure –

Enter FRANCIS. Does he remember the moment at the Woods' House?

FRANCIS	I thought I heard your voice. You're back early.
JAMES	Just this minute in –
FRANCIS	I was there as well.
GINA	Were you?
FRANCIS	You didn't see me, did you?
JAMES	Did I?

,

	No – no, I didn't see you. You didn't see me?
FRANCIS	No, my boy, didn't see *you* at all. Who was in attendance?
JAMES	Oh the Browns, Mr Kasperson, Lord Lewis, you know – I don't remember all the names –
FRANCIS	All the same people as it always was – only now they're high society –
JAMES	Well –
GINA	It's all very grand up there, these days
JAMES	It is –
HEDWIG	Did you play any games?

HEDWIG might react to swearing in the below speech, causing JAMES to emphasise it more.

JAMES	Well, we'd finished our meal, and were having a drink in the library, and they tried to get me to recite some poetry or take their photo but I thought, actually, why should I provide the bloody entertainment on one of the few nights in my life when I'm out for my own enjoyment? They're the ones with the money, all they ever do is trot from house to house stuffing their fat faces: if they want a poem, they can – hire a bloody poet. And if they want their photo taken, that'll be chargeable at the usual rate, thank you very much –
HEDWIG *(wow)*	Did you say that?
JAMES	I gave them a piece of my mind. I said – I hadn't realised I was here, dressed as the entertainment?

The lie (that) to James stood up to (them) when he was in fact humiliated.

GINA	You didn't!
FRANCIS	You said that to their faces!

JAMES implies 'yes I did' without quite saying it.

JAMES	And then there was a whole thing about Chambertin after dinner –
FRANCIS	Chambertin – God, I remember that stuff, Burgundy, isn't it?
JAMES *(no idea)*	It's wine
FRANCIS	Very fine wine indeed –
JAMES	It *can* be a fine wine – but there's a bit of difference between the vintages. Depends on how much sunshine the grapes have had.
GINA	I don't know where you pick this stuff up!
HEDWIG	Did you say that to them as well?
JAMES	It's not a bad lesson for them to learn. However much is written on it, the label isn't all there is to know.
FRANCIS	The idea of you in that place telling them what for. All these years later, my boy is in there. After all that's happened with that crowd.
	,
GINA	Did you really say it to their faces?
JAMES	Yes, but let's not keep talking about it, it was all friendly, they're not terrible people. Why hurt their feelings?

HEDWIG is ingratiating, thoughts of her promised gift.

HEDWIG	I like that jacket, Daddy –

27

JAMES   Do you? And it's the perfect fit – almost like
                 it was made for me – little tight under here,
                 actually, tell you what, let's take it off –

*They help him – it really doesn't fit – he notices something. There's
no carpet visible to the audience at this point.*

                 Carpet didn't come then – or is it an invisible
                 carpet?

GINA   Tomorrow.

JAMES   *That'll* be nice, won't it, Hedwiggicus – your
                 clever old mummy getting us a bargain carpet
                 at the perfect size arriving in time for your
                 birthday – are you excited? I'm excited –

HEDWIG   Dad-dy? –

JAMES   Hed-wig –

She looks at him – as if to say 'Come on' –

                 What?

HEDWIG   You know what.

JAMES   Do I?

                 I don't think I do –

HEDWIG   Stop teasing me! You haven't forgotten, I
                 know you haven't –

He has forgotten.

JAMES   Forgotten what?

HEDWIG   You promised you'd bring me a treat back.

                 Is it in your jacket?

JAMES   No – it's not. But – wait – something even
                 better *is* in my jacket and it's there just for you.

HEDWIG is jumping around. JAMES finds the audience member's jacket and from the pocket, a menu card – properly designed, on thick card.

HEDWIG   Yes – yes – yes!

GINA   Give him a minute!

JAMES   Here it is.

He gives HEDWIG the card.

HEDWIG   It's a piece of paper.

JAMES   No – *wrong* –

HEDWIG   It is –

JAMES   That is the complete menu that lists every
              single dish served tonight.

HEDWIG   Haven't you brought anything?

JAMES   I forgot – but it's not really much of a treat
              having to eat all of these rich foods. You sit
              down and read what it says on the card and
              I'll tell you what each of the courses tasted
              like. Okay?

HEDWIG   Okay.

              I'm not supposed to read at night-time,
              though, am I?

HEDWIG is tearful but tries to hide it. GINA signals to her not to make a fuss, but JAMES notices.

JAMES   For god's sake, it isn't *easy*, having to be at
              these places for the good of the business and
              the good of the name of this household, and
              hold a thousand things in your head at once
              – you forget one little thing and you come
              home to abject misery.

              '

FRANCIS	Good news from the forest, my boy –
JAMES	What?
FRANCIS	She has gone into the basket.
JAMES	Has she?
FRANCIS	She has indeed. Must be getting used to it. But there's a few things to be done, couple of little adjustments we might make. We'll get on with that tomorrow, eh?
JAMES	Absolutely.
GINA	You can't.
JAMES	Why not?
GINA	You've got things to do. You need to sort those family pictures out, the what-were-they-called?, that family with all the children, get the light balanced properly. And there's two of them need combining together – the baby's eyes are red.
JAMES	Are they?
GINA	*Yes,* baby, it won't take long but we promised them a week ago.
JAMES	I said I would do it tomorrow, didn't I? And it will be done tomorrow. Any new orders today?
GINA	No. There are those two sittings here tomorrow but that's all.
JAMES	Am I the only person trying to keep this business going?
GINA	What do you want me to do? I'm putting as many adverts in the paper as we can afford –

JAMES	Has anyone come to view the room downstairs?
GINA	Nope.
JAMES	Well, what can we expect when nobody takes any bloody initiative.
	,
	I'm sorry, Dad, working tomorrow is absolutely what I'll be doing. Day and night. As usual. Working 'til I drop into my grave.
GINA	I didn't mean it like that, and you know it.
HEDWIG	Daddy, do you want a beer?
JAMES	No. No pleasures for me.
HEDWIG	A record on?
JAMES	No.
HEDWIG	Something to / eat?
JAMES	Hang on, wait, did you say a *beer?*
HEDWIG	Yes
JAMES	Is it cold?
HEDWIG	Ice and cold
JAMES	You mean 'ice cold' –
GINA	Go on, go and get it – it'll cheer us up a bit.

HEDWIG heads off for the door. And then suddenly, JAMES gets up from where he's sitting and scoops her up in his arms and kisses her and the two of them end up on the floor.

JAMES	Oh little Hedwig, little Hedwig, I'm sorry – I'm sorry my little duckling, I've been sitting there, stuffing my face at the rich man's table, and I couldn't even – couldn't even bring myself to think

31

JAMES is tearful.

GINA   Stop it –

JAMES   It's the truth. But don't you think forgetting means I love you any less. Because it doesn't. It really does not.

HEDWIG   And we love you, Daddy, the most [that's] possible –

JAMES   And I'm sorry I'm grumpy sometimes, I don't want you to be – I don't want you to have even a speck of negativity in your little life –

              Forget the beer. Shall we … summon the orchestra?

HEDWIG   Yes!

JAMES   Go on then. Well, times are hard, but we are all here together, aren't we, we three? And Grandad. Aren't we, wifey? Whatever anyone else says, better days are coming –

HEDWIG puts a record on and the family dance together. It's interrupted by GINA picking up the microphone:

GINA (m)   And then, a noise downstairs –

              ,

HEDWIG   Who's that?

JAMES   I – don't know –

GINA (m)   It was Gregory Woods, unexpected and uninvited. Carrying a bag.

GREGORY, same clothes as before, but with an outdoor coat on. No bag.

GREGORY   Sorry – I did ring – the front door was open –

GINA   We don't hear the bell from up here –

32

JAMES	Have you left the party?
GREGORY	And my father's house. I'm not sure you recognise me, Mrs Ekdal –
GINA	I do. Of course I do.
GREGORY	I look like my mum – of course – you remember her?
GINA	Do I? Yes, of course – come in.
JAMES	Come in – come in – sorry, you've left the house?
GREGORY	I'll go to a hotel tonight – so *this* is the place –
JAMES	This is the place. This is the studio – this is where the magic happens: where we make memories you can hold in your hot little hand –
GREGORY	The mission command of Ekdal Photography
JAMES *(fast)*	No – City Photography. More neutral, less – foreign-sounding. And anyway, there's a room to rent on the first floor and there's a doctor living by the front door. Now somebody mentioned a beer –

HEDWIG has been standing staring at GREGORY.

HEDWIG	I'll go – I'll go
GREGORY	Hello. I'm Gregory.
HEDWIG	I'm Hedwig.
GINA	Leave that menu here. Read it in the morning, it'll strain your eyes at this time. And put the stairwell light on for yourself.

HEDWIG heads off downstairs.

GREGORY	So that's Heddy. Is she an only child?
GINA	Yes. Spoilt. Like they always are.
GREGORY	She's pretty.
JAMES	She is. The reason she has to have the light on is she's got a condition, her eyes – god, I can hardly get the words out –
GINA	It's muscular degeneration, but Gregory won't [want to know this]
GREGORY	Muscular?

JAMES might find this frustrating.

JAMES	Macular. Macular degeneration. Her retinas. She'll go blind – eventually – I mean, now, she's only showing the first signs, so here's hoping we have a long time before that, but the consultant thinks it's inevitable.
GREGORY	How old is she?
GINA	Thirteen in a day's time –
GREGORY	My god, that's so *young*
JAMES	It's hereditary, probably – that's what they think, now –
GINA	James' mother had it as well –
JAMES	Yes, that's what Dad says – I actually can't remember it at all! But then I was even younger than Hedwig.
GREGORY	The poor thing. Does it frighten her?
JAMES	Oh, she doesn't know.
GREGORY	She [doesn't know]?

JAMES	She's so *happy*, the little songbird, and she's dancing into a life of darkness, endless night. It absolutely breaks my heart – you know, why would you tell her something like that?
GINA	So if you could [keep it under your hat] –

HEDWIG re-enters.

HEDWIG	What? Do you want a sandwich or something, Daddy?
JAMES	That entirely depends what sort of sandwich it is you're offering, Hedwig?
HEDWIG	It's a special sandwich
JAMES	Gregers, will you join me in a special sandwich?
GREGORY	No.

Oddly final, that was.

	I mean, we had that meal, so I'm – I don't need food, thank you.
JAMES	Not too many, waitress. Sit down –

HEDWIG beams and leaves the room. GREGORY sits.

GREGORY	Why is it special?
GINA	It's got no filling – well, it's filled with butter. A lot of butter.
GREGORY	Seeing children always makes me feel old. How long have you two been married now?
JAMES	Twelve years last year.
GREGORY	God – is it?

GINA is suddenly attentive.

GINA	Yes.

35

JAMES   That's right, isn't it?

GINA   Yes!

JAMES   And that whole time you've been – where
                did you say you went?

GREGORY   Away. I spent most of it living – on my own
                – at the top of a mountain.

JAMES   Must have felt like a long time to you?

GREGORY   At the time, it did. Looking back, it feels like
                it passed in a second.

Enter FRANCIS, drunk.

FRANCIS   I wanted to wake, wanted to make a plan for
                tomorrow, for the birthday tomorrow, so I
                thought –

JAMES   Dad – this is Gregory. You might remember
                him. Gregory Woods.

The name panics FRANCIS.

FRANCIS   Woods? Is that the son? What does he want
                with me?

JAMES   He's here to see me, it's okay –

FRANCIS   So nothing wrong?

JAMES   Nothing wrong –

FRANCIS   Not that it would be, of course –

GREGORY goes to him.

GREGORY   Hello, Mr Ekdal.

                We were in a shooting party together once
                – in the summer season, nearly twenty years
                ago. You were a great shot. You helped me, I
                don't know if you remember?

FRANCIS   Army-trained, sah –

GREGORY   Of course. And I used to visit you – at your
                 city house – number 115.

FRANCIS   Beautiful house, that was. Stag's head over
                 the door. Shot him myself.

GREGORY   Yes. You must miss it.

FRANCIS   The house?

GREGORY   The hunting. The great outdoors. Sorry –

*GREGORY, aware that he's caused some discomfort, tries to make it
better and makes it worse*

                 All I mean is how can someone like you *cope*
                 being locked up / here like this – when

FRANCIS   locked up

FRANCIS goes cold. This is awkward.

GREGORY   when when when you're used to the
                 countryside, I mean. The wild. Sorry, you
                 know what I mean.

JAMES steps in.

JAMES   Well, Gregers, there's actually a better way of
                 answering that question than words. See that
                 ladder? Have a look.

GREGORY (m)   Gregory Woods noticed a large ladder,
                 heading up into the attic. He climbed up,
                 put his head through the hatch and peered
                 through it into the loft.

*GREGORY stands on a chair with his head behind the lowered black
curtain –*

GREGORY   It smells like Christmas. Are these – trees?

JAMES   Yes –

FRANCIS	They're cutting down half the trees now, laying cables in the land. The forests are angry. The forests are angry.
JAMES	Can you see anything?
GREGORY	There's moonlight, so –

GREGORY suddenly jumps – maybe we hear wings flapping.

	God – there are pigeons nesting up here! And is that a rabbit hutch!
FRANCIS	It is. Five of them now. Breeding like rabbits.
GREGORY	And there's a bird – in a basket
FRANCIS	Aha! A bird?
GREGORY	Isn't it a duck?
FRANCIS	Is it a duck?
HEDWIG	It's a duck it's a duck it's a duck! But it's not just any old duck –
FRANCIS	Mr Woods, the floor is yours. Please. Say what you see.
GREGORY	It's … brown, I think. It's quite fat.
FRANCIS	But what kind of duck is it?
GREGORY	I don't know.
FRANCIS	That, my boy, is a wild duck.

,

GREGORY	But – it's *here* (?) [i.e. it's not wild]
FRANCIS	It's wild.
HEDWIG	It's my wild duck.
GREGORY	But it lives here?

JAMES	It does. Fresh water every other day for it to swim in, regular gourmet meals courtesy of the Duck-Keeper General here and it's happy as a pig in, uh, a pig-sty.
HEDWIG	It's not a *pig* –
GINA	I think we've maybe had enough nature-watch for one night. It's freezing in here when that thing is open.
GREGORY	Where did a wild duck come from in the middle of a town?
(m)	And scene. In 1884, Henrik Ibsen wrote *The Wild Duck*. His father was a huntsman, so it might be that he had real experience of wild ducks. But the answer to Gregory Woods' question – the origin story of this wild duck was Francis Ekdal's to tell, and had been since it arrived at the Ekdal house some months earlier –
	Sorry, this really is the last time, but we couldn't just borrow that bag – we won't look in it, it's just to be the – you'll see.

GREGORY puts the bag unceremoniously into a big cardboard box that's been onstage since the beginning.

This was six months ago – when Hedwig came up here to find her grandfather sitting in his battered, red-leather armchair with his outdoor coat still on.

A scene begins. FRANCIS' memory and speech are noticeably more fluent here. It could be that he's simply not drunk in this sequence – or it could be something more worrying.

HEDWIG	Grandad –
FRANCIS	Shhh shh shh – where's your mum?

HEDWIG	She's in the kitchen having a coffee and working on those photographs. The problem is that there are too many lines on Mrs Fisher's face and Mr Fisher's eyes are very red so she's re-changing them so they look more like they look.
FRANCIS	Very good, lieutenant. *Now* then.
HEDWIG	What's the box?
FRANCIS	Wait. Look.
	,
HEDWIG	It's moving. The box is moving!
FRANCIS	Is it?
HEDWIG	Did you catch a rabbit?
FRANCIS	Nope. I didn't catch anything.
HEDWIG	Tell me – tell me!
FRANCIS	But are you ready for a story?
HEDWIG	Yes!
FRANCIS	Very good. Once upon a time, humans were out in the wild. And there, we'd have to hunt our own food, track it down and kill it and eat it – and a hunter is a man who feels a deep connection to these ways of old. He roams the fields with a gun in his hand, and his friends by his side, and he *listens* – to the land and the trees, and he follows a scent – the smallest scent – to lead him to his prey. So, this morning, a hunter was out in the deep green countryside, stalking the woods – and he waits and he waits – and then suddenly a fluttering – and quick as a jack-rabbit he whips his shotgun up onto his shoulder and he takes his aim and BANG

he hits her, hit her in flight – a wild duck –

and she falls from the sky

but the hunter's eyes aren't twenty twenty:
he hasn't hit her in the breast, not *here,*
which is where you want to hit to kill the
critter instantly – he hit her *on the wing.* She's
wounded. And here's the thing –

HEDWIG   Was she bleeding?

FRANCIS   Ducks don't bleed, my little peppermint.
[But here's the thing] – the hunter runs up to
where she's fallen, to get a hold of her and
she's ahead of him. She's scuttled fifty feet to
the nearby *lake,* and it's a deep one that lake,
salt-water lake, I remember it well, and into
the water she *dives* –

plunging right down deep to the very, very
bottom. The blue goes green down there, and
then huge, dark, leathery weeds swirling, mud
rising in plumes from the bed of the lake.

HEDWIG   Why? Why has she gone down there?

FRANCIS   This is what a wild duck does when it knows
the game's up. Bottom of the lake, she gets
a beak-full of weeds, hangs on tight and
she waits. She won't ever come up to the
surface again. She's waiting for the air to
run out.

HEDWIG   But she'll die.

FRANCIS   She will.

HEDWIG   Why?

FRANCIS   She was very badly hurt. She knew her life
                 wasn't worth living any more. She took a
                 decision. Sometimes it's the bravest choice
                 you have.

                 ,

He's speaking from his experience. HEDWIG is awe-struck by this.

                 But that's not the end of the story – what
                 animal does a hunter take with him?

Maybe HEDWIG doesn't know so FRANCIS barks for a clue.

HEDWIG   A dog?

FRANCIS   A *dog!* And this hunter has a very clever dog
                 indeed, one that's trained to get after the
                 fallen bird and bring it back to the hunter, so
                 the dog gets on the scent, dives in, swims to
                 the bottom, and he pulls the duck back up.

HEDWIG   Alive?

FRANCIS   Alive. And the hunter takes it back to the
                 house but it doesn't do so well there, only
                 there's a man who works for the hunter who
                 knew me a little bit in another lifetime and I
                 bump into him – and, well, here we are.

*He gestures to the box. HEDWIG lifts the box – and screams with
delight to see the bag – holds it, cradles it, walks around with it –*

GREGORY (m)   And scene.

                 It might be that Henrik Ibsen knew, in 1884,
                 that hunters – even today – think that wild
                 ducks have an instinct for suicide, to dive
                 to the bottom and stay there. But now, this
                 evening, when Francis Ekdal re-told a version
                 of exactly the same story, Gregory Woods
                 started to see another story underneath it,
                 waiting to be brought to the surface –

                 The hunter's my father, isn't he?

FRANCIS	Spot on! What makes you say that?
GREGORY	He was always keen on it –
FRANCIS	I got him into it, my boy, before the – before.
GINA	That duck was shot by Charles Woods? You didn't tell me that.
FRANCIS	You didn't ask me.

,

GREGORY	But it's thriving now, is it, the duck?
HEDWIG	Yes!
JAMES	She's got a bit fat, as you said, but honestly I think she's forgotten what life in the wild was like, and she's happy up there with the rest of us. Though Hedwig lately has been conspiring with the duck to put her back in her box, which must be against some kind of law –
HEDWIG	She likes it in there! All safe and warm –
GINA	The duck does seem to sit in there for hours, sometimes – must be the closed-in-ness, it's like a cuck-oo –
GREGORY	A cuckoo?
JAMES	She means cocoon. You mean cocoon, don't you, Gina?
GINA	Sorry. Yes. Cocoon.
JAMES	Cuckoo! – cocoon! – cuckold! – my wife, and the perils of language!

GINA is embarrassed and deflects the attention –

GINA	Can we have the duck to bed please, Hedwig, and Hedwig to bed too?

FRANCIS	I might have a drink before I turn in, if anyone wants to join?
GINA	You've had a drink
FRANCIS	Have I?

There's a moment of panic before certainty.

> I haven't. Not *tonight*, Gina, love. Permission to retire for the night, lieutenant?

HEDWIG is quite happy to do this routine again.

HEDWIG	Permission granted. Stand down, corporal.
FRANCIS	Permission to kiss the lieutenant on the head?
HEDWIG	Permission granted.

FRANCIS goes out.

FRANCIS	Goodnight, my friend –
GREGORY	Goodnight, Mr Ekdal
GINA	I'm worried about his memory. It's getting worse. And *fast*.
JAMES	He's all right.
GINA	Is he?

It feels like the scene is over. It isn't.

GREGORY	Sorry – you said before you had a room to let –
GINA	The room downstairs, yes, we're advertising it –
GREGORY	Can I have it?
JAMES	You?
GREGORY	Yes. I could move in tomorrow –
GINA	For how long?

GREGORY	Uh, a month, to begin with?
GINA	I mean, it's a small room and it doesn't get any natural light at all –
JAMES	It's a good size room and it gets lots of light from the hall –
GINA	And then there's him downstairs.
GREGORY	Who?
GINA	Relling. Doctor. Out very late, comes back very drunk. And not quietly.
GREGORY	I could get used to that, I'm sure!
GINA	Sleep on it and we'll show you the room tomorrow.
GREGORY	It feels as if you're not keen on me being here, Gina –
GINA (m)	This is true –
GINA	Does it? No, I'm fine –
JAMES	You are being a bit odd. If the man wants to rent the room, the man can rent the room. It's a free country, last time I checked. For the next month, that room is in the name of Gregory Woods.
GREGORY	Don't –
JAMES	What?
GREGORY	I don't like hearing my name – out loud –
GINA	Who does?
JAMES	Oh I don't mind mine – though I suppose, it's *his* really –

GREGORY   But saying it out loud. I'm [Gregory Woods]
               – I mean, can you imagine having to go
               through life being called Gregory Woods?

HEDWIG's interest is aroused and this last question to her, half in play.

               Can you imagine walking around having to
               be Gregory Woods?

HEDWIG   So what would you be if you could be
               anything in the universe?

GREGORY   That is a good question. I think I'd be a dog.

HEDWIG   What?

GINA   Hedwig – bedtime –

GREGORY   I'd be a brilliantly trained, incredibly clever
               dog that could plunge in after a wild duck
               that's dived down to the sea-bed – and drag
               it back out into the air.

               ,

This is weird. JAMES, gleeful at renting the room, breaks the tension.

JAMES   Lives in a dream world! Always did. I have
               to say, Gregers, my old friend, I have no idea
               at all what you're saying with that –

GREGORY   Me neither, really. We'll sort out the details
               in the morning – I'll come back with my stuff
               and – move in. Good night, Gina – Heddy –

GINA   Good night

HEDWIG   Night night

JAMES   I'll show you out – can get a bit dark on
               those stairs –

JAMES and GREGORY go out.

GINA   Wants to be a dog. Course he does.

HEDWIG   I think he meant something else.

GINA   Like what?

HEDWIG   I don't know. But all the time it was like there
                was what he was saying [*she holds up one hand*]
                and then [*the other hand, away from it*] what he
                really meant.

GINA   He's always been a strange one. No wonder,
                with those parents.

JAMES comes back in

JAMES   You see – bit of initiative!

GINA   What do you mean?

JAMES   Gregers letting the room –

GINA   I don't even know where to *start*

HEDWIG   It's good news – it'll be good for us

GINA   I wish it was someone else. What do you
                think Charles Woods will say?

JAMES   He'll say 'what good news!'

GINA   He won't. It's a funny relationship, the two of
                them. It doesn't look good, him moving out of
                the family mansion and coming here. Might
                upset his father. And you don't want Charles
                Woods upset and blaming you.

JAMES   No – God knows he's done enough for us
                over the years. But: rent is money and money
                at a time when we need money. But we won't
                need money for long, Hedwig, will we?

HEDWIG   No!

JAMES   Because soon your father will redeem the
                name of his father and elevate this family,
                lift us out of the – [*can't think of it*] – Lake of
                Despondency –

GINA	It was bedtime some time ago, little lady –
HEDWIG	Can I have a story?
GINA	Do thirteen year olds get stories?
HEDWIG	But I'm not thirteen for… twenty-seven hours.
JAMES	If you're in bed by the time I get there, then maybe –
HEDWIG	Your bed?
GINA	Go on –

HEDWIG kisses her father and goes skidding off to bed. GINA might be about to be annoyed.

JAMES	I want it all for her you know –
GINA	I know
JAMES	Let her be proud to be an Ekdal. Putting right where Dad went wrong.

She kisses him.

GINA	But before that, let's get her to bed.
	Are you asleep?

He is well on the way to being asleep.

JAMES	Am I – ?
GINA (m)	And scene –

The scene dissolves.

[ACT THREE]

GINA (m)	The next morning Gregory Woods moved in. First he set a bath running, but then while moving his things in, locked himself out. Then he tried his other keys, then he comes upstairs to get us to find the spare and let him

in – by which time the bath had overflowed. Gregory Woods then, for some reason, tried to put floor cleaner onto the water. He said he thought it would make it easier to clean up. What it did was make a sort of – swamp of foaming water, which dripped through the light fittings onto the floor below.

JAMES is shifting a sofa into position –

The reason I moved that out of the way is because the carpet is coming later and it can't go down through the furniture, can it?

JAMES   When's it coming?

GINA   Afternoon.

JAMES   It will be back in place by then.

Oh – and Gregers is coming for lunch.

GINA   Today?

JAMES   Yup. Only polite, we can't *not,* can we? I'm sure we've got something in

GINA   Well, we have to have something in, now. Are you going to do those photos?

JAMES   Oh, and Relling's coming too –

GINA   Relling?

JAMES   He came out of his door when I was talking to Gregers on the stairs. What difference does it make, it's *two more people?*

GINA not impressed.

Oh, and Gi-na –

GINA   Ye-es

JAMES   I am trying to stick to the diet –

GINA   The weight loss one?

JAMES   The *weight maintenance* one. It's on the piece
              of paper.

GINA   Sweetheart, I was just [asking] –

FRANCIS appears.

FRANCIS   You busy, son?

JAMES   I am WORKING – if I ever get any peace to
              be able to get some done!

FRANCIS   Very sorry, very sorry – I'm busy as well,
              we're all busy

*FRANCIS storms off; JAMES, exasperated, does too. GINA looks at
the audience.*

GINA (m)   Gina Ekdal had always loved photography.
              You could look at a person through a
              viewfinder and somehow they wouldn't be
              there – you couldn't see them – but then,
              by little adjustments, you suddenly, at a
              certain angle, *had* them – saw them – like a
              bird shooting out of the sky – and that was
              your moment. You were committing to this
              shot – and this shot alone. With the press of a
              button, a million possible pictures fell away –
              and one was held fast in memory. She loved
              that – loved that you could leave things out.
              When she was in town, sometimes people
              would say 'Are you taking a photo of me?',
              and she'd say, 'No, I'm leaving you out of it'.

              What she really loved was film and
              developing the pictures by hand – and
              though technology had moved on, Gina still
              loved the old way. The dark room – a little
              haven that moves at its own … [slow speed]

JAMES reappears with a piece of paper.

What's this?

JAMES   That's my diet, just so it's to hand. And can we get the nice bread?

GINA   Are you busy on the family pictures?

JAMES   I'm *doing it now* –

GINA   Great. Get it out of the way and then later you can *(She quacks.)*

JAMES pulls a face at her. GINA pulls a face back. GINA leaves.

JAMES starts to re-touch some photographs. He produces and then turns on a laptop. It powers up, making a little sound. He opens the photographs. He clicks at it, inexpertly. Looks at the photograph. Little pause. Then from the laptop, he plays some music. Clicks back at the photographs. He really doesn't want to do the photographs.

He switches the music off. He thinks about doing the photographs again. He really doesn't want to do the photographs.

JAMES   Da-ad

FRANCIS   I'm busy.

JAMES makes a sign at his dad through the wall. Eventually FRANCIS comes back in.

I'm not really that busy, in fact.

JAMES   Do you want to go up? Shall I put the ladders up for you?

FRANCIS   Appreciated, appreciated.

JAMES pulls a ladder on castors into place; like library steps. The top of the ladder extends out upwards, out of sight, behind the black curtain. The steps bolt into the floor.

Got to all be ready for tomorrow. It is tomorrow, the birthday, isn't it?

JAMES   Yes indeed it is. And there you are.

FRANCIS climbs up the ladders. From above:

FRANCIS   Not coming?

JAMES   Well –

GINA re-enters, heading out to pick up the food for lunch.

                  no, no, so much to do. Got to do these
                  photographs.

GINA   You haven't forgotten that that couple are
                  coming this afternoon for their portrait shoot –

JAMES   Oh, those two –

GINA   I thought you could sleep after lunch and I'll
                  shoot them –

JAMES   Make sure you clean up afterwards. What?
                  I'm working – I'm sitting here doing it now, I
                  am making these photographs better.

GINA goes. Slight pause. Then, from above:

FRANCIS   I'm just saying –

JAMES   Yes

FRANCIS   I think we will have to move her water-
                  trough

JAMES   I did say that yesterday

FRANCIS   Righteo.

*JAMES carries on working but he's plainly finding the computer hard
to use. HEDWIG comes in. Puts her hands over his eyes from behind.*

HEDWIG   Guess who it is

*JAMES pulls her hands over his shoulders, maybe lifts her over onto
his knee.*

JAMES	You haven't been sent to spy on me, have you?
HEDWIG	No!
JAMES	What's mum doing?
HEDWIG	Gone for food. Can I help you?
JAMES	No, no, must keep dragging the rocks up the hill. Have to keep on working, working till my body bursts like an old paper bag

HEDWIG *(forcefully)* Don't say that. It's not *nice*.

JAMES manages to get the computer to make an error sound. Annoyed, he tries to fix it and it makes the error sound again.

JAMES	I must sit in my seat and play my role as the breadwinner of the household.

He makes it make the error sound again.

HEDWIG	Let me do it.
JAMES	It's not good for your eyes, sweetheart –
HEDWIG	It doesn't hurt them. I promise. I'll do it in no time.
JAMES	But you don't know what I'm trying to do
HEDWIG	You're trying to put *that* on *there*, and then smooth over *that* like *that*, so the whole thing looks nicer
JAMES	Okay.
	But you take responsibility for your own eyes. If it hurts your eyes, you have to say, you have to take responsibility yourself. Yes?
HEDWIG	Ye-es

JAMES	You are the most brilliant, beautiful, intelligent child in the known universe. I'll just be a few minutes.

JAMES goes up to the loft. As HEDWIG works, there's knocking, from above. More knocking. And then GREGORY opens the door, stands in the doorway. HEDWIG's manner of speaking is factual in the way that children often are – she thinks of herself as an adult, but there is an innocence about her lack of irony.

HEDWIG	Hi
GREGORY	Hello.
HEDWIG	You can come in.
GREGORY	Where is everyone?
HEDWIG	Mum's gone to get food and Dad and Grandad are working in the attic.

HEDWIG stops working.

GREGORY	No, don't let me disturb you
	,
	How did the wild duck sleep? Last night?
HEDWIG	Very well, I think. Thank you.
	,
GREGORY	Do you like being in there?
HEDWIG	I do, but to be honest, it's only when I can, because I'm busy.
GREGORY	Because [you have to go to] school?
HEDWIG	Well I used to but then they took me out. Well, my dad did. My mum wanted me to stay but he was worried about my eyes and I had to go and get tested a lot, at the hospital

	– and then we have money troubles and the teachers at my school weren't good teachers – and Dad said I wasn't going back and he'd teach me at home instead and read with me.
GREGORY	So he reads with you?
HEDWIG	Well, he hasn't yet but he's busy.
	,
GREGORY	Tell me about what's up there. With the wild duck.
HEDWIG	There are trees. Old trees. And there's a clock which is called a grandfather clock but it's stopped. And there's quite a lot of books, actually there's one book it's in a different language and – it's got a picture on the front of death so I don't really like to look at it.
GREGORY	Death?
HEDWIG	Yes but he's like a tall skull wrapped up in a big dark shadowy curtain, and he's got an hourglass and a little girl.
GREGORY	And what's going to happen to you? When you're grown up – in the real world?
HEDWIG	This is the real world.
GREGORY	Well, sometimes. But don't you want to see the world out there?
HEDWIG	Probably not. Probably I'll just stay here. I have to look after the wild duck.
GREGORY	Does it not have a name?
HEDWIG	No. It's a *wild* duck. Don't you know what wild means?
GREGORY	I –

HEDWIG	We used to have chickens in there who would have all been family or at least known each other and the rabbits in there are different because probably they do [know each other], but nobody knows the wild duck or knows where she came from or anything.
GREGORY	But it's yours?
HEDWIG	It's mine. Daddy and Grandad can borrow her whenever they want but mainly they just build things for her.
	I feel sad for her because she's been separated from everyone she knows.
GREGORY	And she's been to the very limits. To the deep of the green salt sea.
HEDWIG	Why do you say that?
GREGORY	Well, if you imagine the sea, you imagine the surface. It just looks flat. Like a carpet. Or there – like that piece of paper.

GREGORY lays out a piece of paper, perhaps a photograph.

	But there's more underneath – it goes down and down as far as the sky hangs up.
HEDWIG	I think that's how you speak. Things under the surface.
GREGORY	Do I?
HEDWIG	That's what I think.
GREGORY	Doesn't everything have a meaning kept under the surface? If we're honest. Deeper reasons.
HEDWIG	Like what?
GREGORY	Like why your grandad drinks.

HEDWIG	Why?
GREGORY	You know why. We both do. There's a meaning deep under the surface. The ripples are what you see, but if you dive down… he drinks / because
HEDWIG	Because he went to prison.
GREGORY	Exactly. There it is. Something else under the surface. The deep of the green salt sea.
	What's funny?
HEDWIG	You could just say 'the sea bed'.
GREGORY	Why can't I say 'the deep of the green, salt sea'?
HEDWIG	No, it's just

HEDWIG smiles again.

	It sounds odd to me when other people say that because in my own head I always think of there – up there [the attic] – as 'the deep'. That's what I call it, to myself.
	It's stupid –
GREGORY	It isn't stupid.
HEDWIG	It is because it's just an attic.
GREGORY	How do you know?
HEDWIG	What?
GREGORY	How do you know it's just an attic?
	,
HEDWIG	It's a fact
GREGORY	Is it the truth? Every room is a pocket – it's a little catch of space. A way of shutting things

out. Rooms aren't real. What is a room –
what *is* a room – what is this room?

HEDWIG   A space

GREGORY   A space, right, but space is *space* – space is
                nothing. Walls holding in nothing. What
                does it mean? Really? What's the truth?

*HEDWIG stares at him. She goes to speak – and then GINA comes
in with a tablecloth.*

GINA   You're early –

GREGORY   Apologies –

GINA   No, you have to be somewhere. Table,
                please, Hedwig –

                    ,

GREGORY is unsure what to do here – unusual atmosphere.

GREGORY   Are you taking photographs today?

GINA   Why? Want yours done?

GREGORY   No, thank you. I never quite trusted cameras.

GINA   Because?

GREGORY   I don't know – appearances rather than –
                reality. Maybe.

GINA   It must be difficult, being you.

GREGORY   It is.

                Is it you who does most of the photography?

GINA   We do it together. Anyway it's not really a
                job for someone like James, taking pictures
                of people all day, is it?

GREGORY   No – I suppose not

GINA He's not any old photographer, you know.
I'm probably going to start doing some classes
– people seem to want to learn how to do the
darkroom, the old ways, you know –

A shot is fired from above.

GREGORY What's that?

GINA Hunting.

GREGORY Hunting? How / could it be?

HEDWIG They hunt in the loft. Daddy and Grandad
but mainly Grandad.

*This is said with such normality that GREGORY doesn't know how
to respond. JAMES comes back down the stairs.*

JAMES Hello! Welcome –

The fire alarm starts.

GINA Don't worry – it's them firing that gun – sets
the alarm off –

GINA runs to the back to turn it off. GREGORY continues.

GREGORY Good hunting?

JAMES is embarrassed.

JAMES Oh it's just for Dad, just rabbits –

GREGORY Rabbits? You *shoot rabbits* up there? With a gun?

JAMES Yes, of course with a gun – what else would
we use?

GREGORY A shotgun?

JAMES A handgun.

GREGORY Have you got a licence?

JAMES	Dad does. Did, anyway. But we're at the top of the house, so no one hears him firing it. He hardly ever fires it.
GINA	Men have to have something to abstract themselves with –
GREGORY	What?
JAMES	*Dis*tract themselves with
GINA	That's what I said –
JAMES	Abstract, though, means something different
GINA	Everyone has their own meanings
GREGORY	How's the duck?
JAMES	For someone who's been filled full of shot and dragged around in a dog's mouth, she is in remarkable form
GREGORY	And been down for so long in the deep of the green salt sea –

HEDWIG smiles –

HEDWIG	Yes!
GINA	Come and help me with lunch, Hedwig.
GREGORY	I might go and have a look at her in the daylight –

GINA and HEDWIG leave for the kitchen.

JAMES	I wouldn't watch father when he's in there – not least as he's got that gun. He gets a bit jumpy.
GREGORY	Right
JAMES	I'll show you it later. We've done quite a lot up there. It's a regular little forest for Dad to

roam around in. I used to let him have them in here but Gina didn't like it.

GREGORY   Does she do a lot of the business work?

JAMES   I let her do the more routine things, keeps
            me little slices of time free for strategy and to
            work on other things

GREGORY   Like what?

JAMES   Have I not told you about the invention?

GREGORY   The invention? No –

JAMES   That's the main project these days. We
            started the business for financial reasons, but
            I knew for *me* taking pictures would never be
            enough, not in the long run –

GREGORY   Gina was just saying –

JAMES   So if I was going to dedicate myself to
            photography, how could I make it an *art?*
            And that led to the idea for my invention –

GREGORY   Which is?

JAMES   It takes time to explain. But it'll be ready soon
            – it's not a vanity project, it's a real thing, and
            I can see what I have to do: these days, it's
            funny, my life's work is really pretty clear.

GREGORY   Go on –

JAMES   Him up there. Dad, I mean, not God. I can
            try and repair his self-respect by putting the
            name Ekdal on a real idea. 'Patent pending
            name of Ekdal'. Let him see that there's a
            golden future ahead for us lot when, God
            forbid, he's no longer here.

            What happened to him was – unthinkable,
            really. And that gun up there – don't say

this to him – but that handgun he's got up there has played its own part in the Tragedy of the House of Ekdal. The morning he was sentenced, we were in our old house, his house, you remember, I couldn't find him, it was time to leave for the sentencing, middle of winter, engine was started – and then I hear him: he was in the downstairs bathroom, I had to open the lock with a knife – and he's sitting in there sobbing with that gun in his hand. In my darkest moments I think: maybe he should have just done it. Spared himself. But he didn't dare – already broken then by the publicity, the trial, you know, they really dragged him through the mud.

GREGORY   Yes.

JAMES   The shame. And then that evening, I came back home – alone, he was in custody – alone for the first time in that big house. Knowing it'd be years before he came back.

JAMES stands up – looks around as if looking up in a huge house, on his own.

I'd see people outside in the sunlight, you know, laughing, talking about nothing – it didn't seem real any more. It didn't make any sense. I thought the whole grand parade of life should have *stopped* – stood completely deadly still.

GREGORY   I felt like that – when Mum died. Everything lost its taste. Everything was simulated.

JAMES   Really it was me that was simulated. Inside. I closed all the curtains, pulled down the blinds. For weeks. I walked around that house, walking up and down the stairs, touching every door handle, nowhere to go, no one to live for. And one evening I open the door of the downstairs bathroom and that pistol is still sitting there on the sink – no one else has touched it. Come on, it was saying. Why would you *not?*

,

GREGORY   You didn't [shoot]?

JAMES   No.

              No, I won a significant victory over myself. I kept going. And thank god I did: I met Gina, and then Hedwig and now my invention ... But that choice takes some courage when life is like that.

GREGORY   I guess. It depends how you look at it.

JAMES   You try it. It takes courage.

GREGORY   But it's coming along well? The invention?

JAMES   It's coming along very well.

GREGORY   And the attic isn't a distraction [from your work]?

JAMES   No – on the contrary, I need to rest, sometimes. Often it's when you're relaxing that inspiration strikes – your brain's working away the whole time on how to put the jigsaw together. All the things your eyes see when you don't even realise you're seeing them –

GREGORY (m)   And then I realised something. I realised that on some level, James needed me to help him see.

JAMES   Sorry?

GREGORY   Who is the wild duck?

,

63

JAMES	Who is it? Well, funny you ask that, I'd always thought that the reason Dad had been so keen to keep it is that he felt a sort of identification with it. Wounded, very nearly killed –
GREGORY	It's you. You don't even see it, but he's hit you. And you dropped to the bottom of the lake and you're holding on. You'll die in the dark, green water – it's poisonous.
JAMES	I have no idea what you're talking about –
GREGORY (m)	And scene.
JAMES	Leave *me* out of it, Gregers. If you ever have a family and have to provide for them, you don't have time for – speculation. You have to act.
GREGORY (m)	It was becoming clearer and clearer what had to happen.

GINA and HEDWIG put the lunch down. Another notch up here in naturalism.

RELLING	What a luncheon. A luncheon of kings. Actually, where is the reigning monarch of the house?
JAMES	In the loft. He'll have his later.
RELLING	In which case, let's drink to him – the master hunter – to Lord Francis Ekdal!
JAMES	May his latter days be his happiest days – and welcome, Gregers!
RELLING	So when did the junior Mr Woods descend from on high?
GREGORY	I moved in this morning, if that's what you're asking.

RELLING	I remember you. Very right on, if memory serves. Or should I say, very left[-wing] on. You worked for your dad, didn't you?
GREGORY	Yes
RELLING	In the warehouse, walking among the people. Work your way up from the bottom. And most of his free time was spent trying to sign his father's workers up to the revolution. Not entirely successfully.
GREGORY	Not at all successfully
RELLING	Growing up is the process of adding water to the wine of your dreams.
GREGORY	Not if you're pouring for someone with a true palate –
	,
RELLING	Too much wine and even the sommelier gets drunk.
GREGORY	Meaning?
RELLING	In all things, moderation. Add water.
GINA	You were in late last night again, speaking of moderation –
JAMES	Can I have the butter?

HEDWIG gets the butter for him. It's a butter dish – he opens it: no butter.

RELLING	I was hoping you'd hear me – it was all an act, designed to get your attention, Gina
GINA	If this is supposed to be flirting
RELLING	You're a lucky man, James Ekdal. All the butter you can eat. A forest above your head

with its own noble old custodian. A beautiful
wife beside you, holding the fort, while
you make ready to unleash your glorious
invention on an unexpectant world –

GINA   And Hedwig –

RELLING   And Hedwig!

HEDWIG   And the wild duck!

RELLING   I come up those stairs and I am wracked with
            envy – if I had been him [James], the things I
            would have done – the luckiest / man in the
            world

GREGORY   Oh come on – if my dad hadn't thrown his
            dad under the bus, we'd be eating this meal
            in a mansion.

JAMES   Gregers, I won't to hear a word against your
            dad. He's been good to me.

GREGORY   And you're not even the people worst off –
            there are people he's sacked from the bottom
            rungs of the company who are a feather
            away from the street – taking hand outs to
            even have food on their table –

RELLING   I don't actually understand what you're
            preaching –

GREGORY   That the water is rising. That there's going
            to be a change. A major change which will
            force us to open our eyes.

RELLING   God, this again –

GREGORY   Ideals, you mean? Integrity?

RELLING   That's not what I would call it –

GREGORY   I think we had this conversation years ago

RELLING   I think we did too. And I'll ask you now what
              I asked you then. When you've demolished
              the corrupt, patriarchal, capitalist system, what
              are you going to do? What happens next?
              Start a new world order in innocence and the
              spirit of human nobility like the Garden of
              bloody Eden? People will still be people.

GREGORY   And people like my father will still have
              people like us under his thumb.

RELLING   And people like you never have a fucking
              clue – pardon my language – never have a
              clue about how to actually get anything *done*
              in the real world, with real, ordinary people
              who don't have the luxury of living in ideals.

GREGORY   And you do?

RELLING   Accredited thorassic surgeon. If your illness
              was in your chest and not in your head, I
              could crack your ribs open and cut it out for
              you.

GREGORY   But – you no longer practice?

RELLING   No need for practise when you're really,
              really good. Salt, please.

Down comes FRANCIS with a dead rabbit and a real gun.

FRANCIS   Good afternoon, all, very successful
              morning's hunting – bagged a biggun – Gina,
              I'm going to pop it in the kitchen and I'll
              skin it later on –

Out he goes.

GINA   Put it in the sink – Francis, please! It's a tiny
              kitchen, and he wrecks it with those things.
              Destroys it. Blood all over the place. Put it in
              the sink!

GREGORY	That's not ideal –
RELLING	Is anything?
JAMES	Not in the Ekdal family. Not so far, at least. But we must keep on working, ey, Hedwig?
HEDWIG	Yes!

GINA has spotted the cardboard box, sitting conspicuously.

GINA	Heddy, is there a duck in that box?
HEDWIG	She *likes* it in there –
GINA	Can she *please* stay upstairs, James –
JAMES	Hedwiddikins, I want a solemn promise that the duck will be back in her basket before the afternoon's over –
HEDWIG	I promise.
JAMES	Promise promise?
HEDWIG	Promise promise.
JAMES	Doesn't miss a thing, this one – come here!
RELLING	You still working for the company?
GREGORY	Not really.
RELLING	And Woods & Son will one day all be yours.
GREGORY	Hopefully not.
RELLING	Someone wouldn't drink his daddy's Kool-Aid
GREGORY	I don't drink poison. For you or for him.
JAMES	God, not this again –
RELLING	Alcohol's a poison. When will I die? Who knows. Am I *happy?* As much as I can be, given circumstances.

JAMES	Right, Gregers, here's a story you'll like. My dad had to have an operation a year or so ago, nothing major, but at one point he needed a blood transfusion. Unexpectedly. And I actually have quite a rare blood type – must be from my mother – so I couldn't, or obviously I would have done it, but Hedwig here is a direct match. Anyway – she agrees to give blood to Grandpa, so she says goodbye to her mum, big hug, we go into the room and they wash her arm and then she's sitting there with the doctor, with the thing coming out of her arm, giving blood to her granddad. Solemn little face. 'You're being very brave', the doctor says. 'I know but when you love someone, what can you do?', she says. Doctor's a bit taken aback by that. Then Hedwig looks at me, vulnerable – 'Dad', she says, 'am I going to die tonight or tomorrow?'

,

And my heart just

He mimes his heart exploding.

GREGORY	That is beautiful.
HEDWIG	You're teasing me – *again* –
GREGORY	It really / is beautiful, Hedwig –
JAMES	No, I am *celebrating* you because you are a pure, gorgeous little goddess – and I am practising celebrating you because what day is it tomorrow?
HEDWIG	Stop it –
JAMES	But I tell you what, you deserve a million times more than I can give you. A small party in the loft. A meagre little party in a loft. I mean –

The mood could drop here – HEDWIG knows how to buck him up.

HEDWIG   I'm excited!

She puts her arms round his neck.

RELLING   You just wait for this invention. You just wait,
                Heddy. The things you'll have then.

JAMES   Oh you shall want for *nothing* – you'll have
                [he can't think of it] – *anything* you want –
                and that will be my reward for years of toil
                and trouble and toil

HEDWIG   I love you

*HEDWIG squeezes him. There's a little pause. RELLING addresses
GREGORY.*

RELLING   I like your daddy. Sir Charles. Good man.

GREGORY   He's not a sir. And he's not a good man.

RELLING   And that's your contribution to this lovely
                family atmosphere!

GREGORY   It's a poisoned atmosphere.

                              ,

GINA   What is? The windows have been open all
                morning –

RELLING   The only poison round here comes out of
                your mouth –

JAMES   Gentlemen, gentlemen –

GREGORY (m)   And scene –

                A few minutes later / the

*As the others make to leave, RELLING breaks the convention, grabs
hold of GREGORY.*

70

RELLING   Don't try it on them. Oy. Listen. Don't. Try.
               It. Here.

GREGORY   Try what?

RELLING   Smashing the reality of the mind into the
               reality of the world.

GREGORY   What if I do?

RELLING   Then I will kick you down all three flights of
               stairs and out of the fucking door.

               ,

               I see you. And I see how you look at the girl

GREGORY is winded by this

GREGORY   I would never lay a finger / on Hedwig –

RELLING   It's the idea, though, no?

RELLING goes

               ,

GREGORY (m)   A few minutes later, the bell rings. It's my
               father. He wants to speak to me, my room's
               still full of water – so we have to speak in
               here.

CHARLES and GREGORY alone.

CHARLES   You said some things last evening. And your
               moving in here suggests to me that you're
               fixating on something I did – or said. I was
               worried.

GREGORY   I'm here because I don't want to stay in your
               house. Well, actually this *is* your house, isn't
               it, it's been a sort of doll's house little-theatre
               for you to play your games, hasn't it, but I
               have something I need to do here

CHARLES	Which is?
GREGORY	Which is *open their eyes*
CHARLES	And so why the aggression to me? It's not because of me their eyes / are closed [whatever you mean by that].
GREGORY	I feel guilty *all the time.* And that is because of you. I have your name written on me – written *through* me like a stick of rock –
CHARLES	Why do you feel guilty?
GREGORY	I should have stood up to you then. I should have warned Francis Ekdal. I shouldn't have let it happen, I should have told him to mount his own case – and not let a sweet man go to jail. He is *broken.*
CHARLES	Perhaps you should. Why didn't you?
GREGORY	Because I was frightened of you. Terrified.
	,
CHARLES	Well, it seems that fear has passed –
GREGORY	[But] too late for me to put things right. With the father. He's too far gone. But I can put things right for his son. I can show him the invisible lies that tie his hands together so that he can get himself free –
CHARLES	Greg. Please. Honestly – really honestly – do you think that will do any good?
GREGORY	It will (!) – OF COURSE IT WILL
CHARLES	If I hadn't helped them, they'd have been in dire straits –

GREGORY   And maybe they'd have found their *own*
            way. I know what you've done here, Dad. I
            know what you've done.

CHARLES   You really think James Ekdal is the kind of
            person who's going to thank you for doing
            this to him?

GREGORY   He is *exactly* that kind of person, yes –

CHARLES   I disagree –

GREGORY   I would rather shoot myself in the head than
            do nothing and have to live with feeling like
            this –

CHARLES   You've always felt like this, you've *always* felt
            like this

GREGORY   Have I?

CHARLES   Yes – this is who you've always been. And
            it's not your *fault*, Gregory, it's not your fault
            – you had a parent with a serious mental
            illness –

GREGORY   That is absolutely true –

CHARLES   I meant / your mother, as you know
            perfectly well –

GREGORY   And I meant *you*.

CHARLES   And paranoid, over-heated conversations
            like this one are your inheritance from her
            – one thing she did leave you –

GREGORY   He's still bitter about the life insurance!
            Sixteen years later! Married her for the
            money and the dead bitch didn't pay out –

*CHARLES loses it momentarily, a real flash of rage, grabs his son
by the throat – GREGORY is frightened of him, doesn't respond –*

CHARLES	*I am not going to justify myself to you, Gregory:* I will not do it.
	I hope, I really hope you never have to understand what it was like, when the person you love gets ill – that you never have to watch the person you love slowly fall into total confusion.
GREGORY	So you think you *loved* her?
CHARLES	Shall we keep to the point in hand? You seem certain of your course of action here.
GREGORY	I am.
CHARLES	Then I shouldn't have bothered coming. You'll always have a home at / my house
GREGORY	I'm not coming back.
CHARLES	And as for the business, [I presume]
GREGORY	It's a no from me.
	And you can take me off the payroll. Dismantle my stockholding. I don't want anything to do with it. It's a sack of bricks. I don't want any of it.
CHARLES	You don't / want any – ?
GREGORY	No.
CHARLES	How are you going to live?
GREGORY	I have savings.
CHARLES	And how long are they going to last?
GREGORY	Long enough. They'll last me out.

'

CHARLES	What do you mean by that?

GREGORY   No more questions. Go home.

GREGORY picks up the microphone, momentum building – CHARLES exits –

(m)   In 1884, Henrik Ib –

                 I'm just going to speak for myself.

                 There are times when there are rights and
                 there are times when there are wrongs, and
                 we pretend that it's all grey area, all in the
                 middle. And why? Because we tell ourselves
                 the lies and we tell ourselves the lies and
                 we say the things that we're supposed to
                 say – we let the toxic people, the cancerous
                 personalities continue, continue spooning the
                 poison into our water, we turn a blind eye –
                 no, our eyes *are* blind to it: we look without
                 seeing, deny that it even *happens,* saying 'but
                 it's their business', 'not to do with me', and
                 then at a certain point, on some afternoon
                 in the middle of a mouthful of a dinner, we
                 WAKE THE FUCK UP – and we SEE that
                 this isn't *good,* this isn't *right,* that it's nothing
                 to do with politeness, we see how injustices
                 invisibly persist, and we *see* that a lie can
                 just *grow* like a tumour – and then we are
                 the doctors and it becomes our mission, to
                 do what it takes, to *risk* ourselves, to gamble
                 our social standing, to cut free, to change the
                 story, forget what people might think – and
                 say: *stop*

He takes a breath –

                 James!

*JAMES enters – hurriedly – GINA and HEDWIG and RELLING after
him – GREGORY slams the mic down (or into RELLING's hand)
grabs JAMES's jacket and throws it to him –*

75

	We need to go for a walk. The two of us. Now.
JAMES	What's happened? What did your dad want?
GREGORY	Here – come on

GREGORY sweeps out of the front door –

RELLING	He's off his head –
GINA	James, his mother was the same – I said to / you
JAMES	I'm his *friend* – okay? I'm his friend.

JAMES goes after him.

RELLING	Dogs that sick should be put down.
GINA	Do you really think he's ill? Gregers?
RELLING	It's more serious than physical illness –
GINA	What do you think it is?
RELLING	Severely inflamed sense of victimhood leading to uncontrollable presentations of how virtuous he is. He's a sick puppy.
GINA	He's always been strange. When I first met that family, he was strange.

GINA heads back into the kitchen. RELLING stands alone onstage. Picks up the bottle of wine left on the lunch table. RELLING surveys the audience.

RELLING (m)	Time for a drink.

RELLING puts the microphone down. The house lights rise. As the audience start to applaud, and RELLING leaves, HEDWIG enters, hurriedly –

HEDWIG	WAIT WAIT WAIT – hang on – wait –
	If I said I would, then I have to, otherwise that's lying –

76

Hello duck – I'm going to open the box now, okay?

HEDWIG opens the box. In it, like magic, a real duck.

How are you?

HEDWIG picks the duck up.

Yes, you *look* well –

My eyes are a little bit sore today but otherwise I'm fine.

Exit HEDWIG, carrying duck –

[INTERVAL]

In the interval, the space stays live. A carpet is delivered and laid. GINA hoovers it, and then sets about developing, by hand, a series of photographs, which are hung on a line at the very back.

[ACT FOUR]

As the interval ends, GINA finishes a job and picks up a microphone. HEDWIG sits at the table, waiting – and very slowly, the house lights go down –

GINA (m)   He was never late for dinner. Only today, he was. An hour after the normal time, the table was ready, the bread was cut and he –

JAMES enters. (This section fast).

HEDWIG   DADDY! We waited for you and waited – where have you been?

GINA   You've been a long time, James.

JAMES   Have I?

GINA   Did you have dinner with Gregers?

JAMES   No.

77

JAMES hangs up his coat. GINA to HEDWIG:

GINA   Right, sweetheart, let's get this show on the
                  road –

JAMES   I don't need food. I don't want food.

HEDWIG   Are you ill?

JAMES   I'm fine. I had a punishing walk, that's all.

GINA   You should be careful, Jamesy, don't do too
                  much –

JAMES   Any new orders while I was out?

GINA   Not today, no –

HEDWIG   There will be tomorrow, Daddy, wait and
                  see – there will be

JAMES   Tomorrow's when the work really starts for
                  me.

HEDWIG   Not tomorrow – remember what tomorrow is –

JAMES   Well, the day after tomorrow. Because then,
                  I am going to manage my business myself,
                  hands on, just me, on my own.

                  ,

GINA   But you have to work on your invention /
                  and

JAMES   Don't talk to me about that –

HEDWIG   But Daddy, you have to help me look after
                  the wild duck –

JAMES bangs the table or something

JAMES   I don't want to ever see the wild duck again.

HEDWIG   She *needs* you –

JAMES	Hedwig, *enough*
HEDWIG	And we're having my *party* tomorrow – you'll *have* to see her –
JAMES	I will go into that loft and I will take the wild duck and I will wring her fucking neck.

,

It's now clear that something is seriously wrong. HEDWIG looks to GINA who is looking at JAMES.

HEDWIG	But it's *my* wild duck –

,

JAMES	And that is the only reason I will spare its life. Because I should take anything – *anything* from this house that has been in *his* hands and I should *burn it* –
GINA	James, what is going on?
JAMES	There are certain things – certain – certain principles, certain ideas that are – *necessary* for someone to feel worth *anything,* for a marriage to – to be a marriage there are certain ideas, that are essential, that cannot be *broken.*
HEDWIG	But Daddy, the poor wild duck –
JAMES	I won't touch a hair on its head. Okay? I said that. Now – you're going to be a good little duckling and go into your bedroom for a minute so I can talk to your mum.

,

Have you put your [eye] drops in?

HEDWIG	No.

JAMES	Right then.
HEDWIG	You won't go up there and hurt her when I'm gone –
JAMES	I promise I won't.
HEDWIG	Promise promise
JAMES	Promise promise

HEDWIG goes, but then turns – and rushes back at her dad – and hugs him. He gives into it. Then:

Go on.

HEDWIG goes.

GINA	James, what's / wrong?
JAMES	From tomorrow I'll be doing the accounts myself. Here, in the house.
GINA	What is this about? *Why* would you / want to –
JAMES	Because I want to know where the money is coming from.
GINA	Well, that won't take long. There's hardly any of it.
JAMES	I want to see how so little money can stretch so strangely far –
GINA	Hedwig and I don't need very much –
JAMES	Would you say it was true that my father is paid – and generously paid – by Charles Woods for the accounts work or stocks or whatever it is he's doing?
	,
GINA	I wouldn't say it was generous but he's paid.

JAMES	And is it true that you know that I didn't know that –
GINA	It pays his way and very little more –
JAMES	It pays his way – but you *knew* that I took pride in being able to look after my dad – you do *know* that, because I have *said* that –
GINA	I don't know why you're getting so upset –
JAMES	Because Woods's money is secretly leaking into my family and my wife is keeping his secrets –
GINA	Don't shout at me.
	We don't know if Woods even *knows* about your Dad's money, it could just be that secretary, whatever his name was, his people, someone else who knew your dad back in the day – I don't understand why it matters –
JAMES	Your voice has gone funny. I'd like to put a light on.

GINA puts a lamp on.

GINA	I didn't get your dad his job; if you really want to know, it was Anna. Her suggestion. I knew it made you happy to look after him and I didn't want to spoil your happiness for nothing. So you can stop being angry with me.
JAMES	I think your hands are shaking.
GINA	Are they?
(firm)	Okay, what has he said about me?
JAMES	Who?
GINA	Gregory. Mad Gregory. Seriously. Spit it out. Tell the truth.

JAMES	Could it be true – could it be true that you and Mr Woods conducted some sort of relationship, in the period when you were his employee?

This is huge. GINA's reaction is not explosive – at all – and lasts only the smallest fraction of a second before she plays it down.

GINA	Oh – that.
	No. No, James, that isn't true.
JAMES	No?
GINA	No. I told you. You know this story. His wife thought there was something going on and there was a whole thing, calling me at night, one time she turned up at the flat, screaming and screaming, pulled out a clump of my hair, actually – but, really what that was, was that she was crazy. Medically crazy. Like her son. This was years ago, I was still in my twenties. But that whole thing is one of the reasons I put my resignation in.
JAMES	And that's it?
GINA	Yes.
	No
	He came to see me afterwards at home. To apologise for his wife. He brought me flowers. And – one thing led to another – it was inevitable, really, I mean, we'd –
JAMES	What?
GINA	When someone else says that it's already *happened* between two people, it creates a – I don't know, a *charge,* when people think – it's what people think – there's an idea of it now. And he came to the house and his wife

	had gone into the hospital by then, and he was lonely and he wanted me and I didn't know how to say no.
JAMES	So he forced you?
GINA	It wasn't – no, he didn't – but we weren't thinking.
JAMES	And we were together then. You and me.
	,
GINA	Yes. It didn't *mean* anything, we weren't thinking –
JAMES	And that was the only time the two of you –
GINA	No.
JAMES	How many times?
	How many times?
GINA	Three.

GINA picks up the microphone.

(m)	More than three.

GINA leaves and heads somewhere else in the room.

	Do you want a drink?
	,
JAMES	Of course you realise what you've done. It's – my own home, my own life is just completely poisoned. Has been for years. For years and years.
GINA	And what exactly would have happened to you? What would you *do* if you didn't have me?
JAMES	What does that mean?

GINA	The rages. The drinking. The moods. When I met you, you were totally off the rails: half-child, half-wild, your father in prison – and look at you now: you're a parent, a married man, a *different man*, you've become who I always knew you *were* –
JAMES	Well, I'm sorry you don't know what it's like to feel sad –
GINA	I know what it's like – I KNOW WHAT IT'S LIKE.

,

Are you not going to eat?

JAMES lifts up the butter dish. There's real butter in it. He looks at it, almost tearful.

(m)	And scene –

JAMES snatches the microphone from GINA's hands and destroys it.

JAMES	NO.
	No. We *have* the conversation. We have the fucking conversation. We made vows to each other. I am entitled to know the truth about my own life. You owe me the truth. Why? Why did you do that to me?

,

GINA	I don't know –
JAMES	I wasn't enough.
GINA	*No* –
JAMES	Well?

,

GINA	I don't know –

Slight feeling that GINA doesn't know what to say here, as if we've run out of script and JAMES is pushing us into new territory.

JAMES	So, to be absolutely clear, the truth is: when we were – first – when we first – when we first were *with each other*, you were also – with him?
GINA	No – it wasn't like that –
JAMES	How was it?
GINA	James –
JAMES	No, *please,* tell me how it was
GINA	I came back. I chose you. You won –
JAMES	I can't tell you how happy that makes me –
GINA	I missed you. I missed the excitement of each new day – with you. I thought about it and the idea that I wouldn't get to do the next things with you and choose furniture and *carpets* and make a home and have a child – I couldn't bear that, I couldn't bear that all that time we'd put behind us together would all just crack apart. I didn't want that. That wasn't what I wanted.

GINA might wish she had a microphone at this point. But there isn't one.

JAMES	You should have told me.
GINA	You're right.
JAMES	So – WHY?
GINA	Because –
	I thought you'd leave me. I couldn't throw my life away.

JAMES	God all of it – everything – my home – all of it I owe to that gnarled, old, rutting, rapist – it's all *HIS,* I could rip his eyes out – god what have you *done* to me?

JAMES sends a chair flying.

GINA	James, this is crazy, this is ancient history. You can't regret the time we've had together –
JAMES	I've lived for fifteen years, every day, every single second, in a web of lies and secrecy and eaten my dinner without realising that there are little bodies buried in every fucking inch of my home. If you want to talk about regrets, surely – *surely* – we are talking about *you.*
GINA	I –
	I'd forgotten. I'd made myself forget it ever happened.
JAMES	Keep your eyes down. Hope it goes away. Who else knows?
GINA	Nobody – I didn't think about it – I don't think about it –
JAMES	Like an animal that's got used to the poison.
GINA	Stop it James, just – you're not a child. I know it was wrong. I know it was wrong, and it wasn't fair, but I have given you a *lot* – I hold this house together. I keep this whole thing going, I keep the whole thing going. I give you the space for your work, I support your invention – I am a good wife and a good businesswoman and a good mother. A really, really good mother – better than yours and better than mine and better than Gregory Woods's
	,

I'm sorry. About –

I didn't ever want to make you unhappy.

GREGORY enters.

GREGORY   I know this is hard. But – the truth will set
            you free. And Hedwig will be free from lies.
            You can start again. In truth. With everything
            brought out into light.

GINA takes a shade off a light.

GINA   That better?

GREGORY   Gina, I didn't mean to –

GINA   Those old stories were *gone*. And you have
            brought them here. So now might be a great
            time to shut the fuck up.

JAMES   This is the worst day of my life.

GREGORY   But there is another way of understanding
            this, James – of starting anew

GINA   Gregers –

RELLING   Thought as much.

RELLING's come in. To the implied 'what?'

            The wild ducks are flying around again.

JAMES   The victims of Mr Woods.

RELLING   Who are?

JAMES   Some of us have been for a long time,
            Relling, but we only found out today.

RELLING looks at GREGORY. He realises what's happened.

RELLING   What are you trying to do?

GREGORY   I'm sorry?

87

RELLING	What are you trying to do?
GREGORY	I'm trying to allow them to have a real marriage. An honest marriage.
GINA	It's our marriage –
RELLING	Not good enough for you as it was?
JAMES	Relling, I'm not sure you understand –
RELLING	How many real, honest marriages have you come across in your life, Mr Woods?
GREGORY	I'm not sure I've ever encountered one.
RELLING	Me neither. Funny that.
JAMES	You wouldn't know, Relling, because it's morality, it's a moral foundation, it's basic right and wrong, truth and lies. It's not some abstract thing: it's the ideals by which we stay alive. It's the world underneath your feet. He's [GREGORY] done me a favour.
RELLING	I'm sure. I'm not going to stay for this. And you two can do whatever you like with your marriage. End of the day, no one else cares. But I'll tell you this for free: Hedwig is *thirteen*. And she is as much a part of your marriage as the two of you – and a damn sight more than he [GREGORY] is. She's soft mud, she's open to any impression. She's innocent here. Be gentle with her. She'll be easy harmed.
GINA	She's twelve. Hedwig. She's / twelve
ANNA	I'm sorry, I rang the bell but no one –

ANNA comes in. She's older, wiser. She's younger than CHARLES, maybe the right age to have been GREGORY's mum. An immediate charge between her and RELLING.

Is this a bad moment?

GINA   – no, no, it's fine

ANNA   Oh, I like the carpet –

GINA   Yes! We're very happy with it. Came this
                afternoon.

ANNA   Well, we're pleased you're pleased with it. It
                looks right here: I told you it would.

JAMES looks at GINA. The carpet story was a lie.

GINA *(quick)*   What can we do for you, Anna?

ANNA   Well, I wanted to bring Heddy's present over
                for tomorrow – Charles is away now, until
                [next week] – but it's from both of us –

GINA   You're always so generous –

JAMES *(mocking)* From both of you?

GREGORY   They're getting married.

No one sure of whether GREGORY is joking – this is new news.

ANNA   Yes. Yes we are.

GINA   Oh that is such good news, Anna – at *last* –
                congratulations, really. I'm so happy for you
                – for you *both* –

ANNA is looking at RELLING.

ANNA   Me too.

RELLING   Are you telling the truth?

ANNA   I am.

RELLING   So you want to get married again?

ANNA   That's what I said

RELLING   Working for Charles all these years, you'll
                know exactly how plush a wedding he can
                afford –

89

ANNA	Nothing big, nothing fancy.
RELLING	Well it has to be better than your first try. *(To GREGORY.)* Your dad's not a big drinker, is he? And as far as I've heard, he doesn't go around beating his wives up. So already a significant improvement on Anna's dear departed first husband.
ANNA	My first husband had his better parts too, John.
RELLING	I'm sure.
ANNA	And he didn't let his go to waste.

,

RELLING struggles to find a response to this. When he can't: self-destruct.

RELLING	James – I'm going to hit the town tonight. Hard. I'm going to drink until I go temporarily blind and I'm sick in my own mouth. Fancy coming?
ANNA	Oh, don't do that, John. Please don't – / let's just
RELLING	Well – what else is there?

RELLING goes, slamming the door. No one really knows what to make of that.

ANNA	Yes, there is a history there. There was a time when –
GREGORY	Which I'm sure your future husband knows all about –
ANNA	Of course he does. We tell each other everything. Anything that anyone could say about me – any true thing, at least – I've told him. And he's done the same for me.

ANNA looks at GINA, no malice at all.

GINA   That's – wonderful.

ANNA   It really is. It's a bit of a – relief. We're like a
            pair of kids together, embarrassingly honest
            and open and *happy*. And that's a first for
            both of us.

GREGORY   A first?

ANNA   He's a good man, your father, whatever you
            think of him. He's worked a long life, and spent
            too many years being the target of someone
            else's rage – his father's [rage] when he was a
            boy, and your mother's most of his adult life.
            And from what I can see, his crimes have very
            often been committed only in someone else's
            imagination. I'm not criticising her, Greg, she
            was ill and she couldn't help it – but at the same
            time, it doesn't mean it's the life *he* deserved.

GREGORY   'In sickness and in health' was the vow he
            swore, I think. You've got that coming. Though
            I presume you're more focussed on the 'death
            do us part' section … spousal inheritance being
            / what it is –

ANNA   You can disapprove as much as you like. But if
            you want to talk about sickness, I don't notice
            his son coming in to calm his fears and care for
            him, the outlook being as it is –

GINA   What outlook?

GREGORY   It doesn't matter –

ANNA   There's no point trying to hide it. He's going
            blind.

JAMES   Going [blind]? Your father? Gregers, you
            didn't say [anything] –

GREGORY	I didn't know –
ANNA	He's been diagnosed now: it's a specific condition –
JAMES	Macular degeneration
ANNA	Yes – that's it –

,

A silence roars. Things suddenly become clear.

GINA	It happens to lots of people
ANNA	But my eyes will have to do for the both of us. Anyway. I'll do what I came to do, and I'll put this here for Heddy, in the morning.
GINA	Thank you

She puts a present down, which is better wrapped than the others. And an envelope.

ANNA	And this, too. This is the more important thing. Don't let her rip it open in excitement. Right. We were sorry not to see you to say goodbye the other night, James. I'm sorry about Charles' friends. Pompous sacks of self-regard, the lot of them.
JAMES	Tell your husband that I will come to see him to discuss the payment of my debts. That the key thing sustaining me as I work on my invention is the hope that one day I will be able to give back every last penny and stand on my own two feet.
ANNA	I'm not sure what's happening here, but I'm going to go. Give Heddy my love.

She goes. A long silence.

Then, genuinely dangerous, JAMES moves to the letter ANNA has just put down

GINA   James, what are you doing?

JAMES has opened the letter addressed to HEDWIG. And reads it. There's a few different pieces of paper inside.

                  That's *her* birthday present –

JAMES   I know exactly what it is, thank you, I do not need you to paint me a picture.

JAMES reads. A pause. Then:

                  Do you know what this says?

GINA   How could I?

JAMES   Do you *know* what this *says*?

GINA   NO

JAMES   It is documentation that a trust has been set up, from which the sum of one thousand pounds will be paid to Hedwig Ekdal on a fortnightly basis for the rest of her life, including a pretty fucking huge lump sum on her eighteenth birthday –

                  ,

GREGORY   This is a trap, James –

JAMES shuts GREGORY down.

JAMES   I don't need help, thanks, Greg, I am fully, *fully* aware of what is going on here. I can – in fact – *see*. And however little you both think of me, I'm not a man who can be bought.

JAMES rips the piece of paper neatly in two. GREGORY didn't predict this next development – didn't see it himself.

	So much for that. But we haven't had the truth yet, have we, Gina? It's not the first time your father has put money into this household – Gregers, as you've already told me, he's pouring money into my father's pocket.
GINA	James –
JAMES	He is *paying* my dad. Overpaying him. Maybe paying him *for nothing*. Has done for years. My dad is living off *his* money. That's true –
GINA	Yes.
JAMES	And – another generous gift – he put up almost all of the money for our wedding –
GINA	Yes.
JAMES	So – wait – if you and he were together just as we were getting engaged, why would he – why would he pay for you to get married? Why would he want to do that?
GINA	Honestly?
	I think he thought he could come and – *have* me whenever he wanted.

JAMES momentarily shocked –

JAMES	And is that / what's been – ?
GINA	No – no, I haven't, please god I wouldn't do that to you – nothing has happened since then. There hasn't been any physical contact at all, James, I promise, nothing has happened since the day we were married.
JAMES	I don't think that's why he paid for the wedding. I think that the truth of it is that he was worried about something else.

GINA	I don't understand –
JAMES	She doesn't need *this* [the letter] because Hedwig's already got her inheritance from him, hasn't she? *Here. (He violently gestures at his eyes.)*
GINA	James, I don't understand –
JAMES	Does your child have the right to live in this home? In *my* home?
GINA	Oh *Jesus Christ* –
JAMES	Is Hedwig mine?

GINA smacks JAMES hard across the face.

GINA	How dare you ask me that –
JAMES	Is. Hedwig. Mine?

,

GINA is unhysterical. Almost hard.

GINA	I don't know.

,

JAMES	You don't know. But there are tests / and
GINA	I didn't – I haven't done that – and I don't know.

,

JAMES	Right.
	Then I have to get out of here. There's no way I can stay in this house.

JAMES heads over to get his overcoat and puts it on. A sudden whirl of activity –

GREGORY	James, the three of you have to stay *together* now – you have to *forgive her*
JAMES	No I don't – and no I don't – for fuck's *sake*, you heard what she said –
GINA	Please don't do this
GREGORY	*James* –
JAMES	I don't have a daughter – I *don't have* a daughter –
HEDWIG	Daddy?

,

Everyone realises a tearful HEDWIG's in the room. And she heard that. JAMES is distraught, can't face her, moves first for the door – she runs to grab hold of him, he fights her off, it's pretty ugly and probably requires quite a bit of ad-lib –

JAMES	I can't, Hedwig, I can't – don't look at me – get off, get off me, get off me, I can't bear it, I can't bear it, I can't bear it – I have to get out –
GINA	James, look at her – look at her –
HEDWIG	Daddy – daddy – daddy – please

…until JAMES is gone.

HEDWIG is in tears, GINA is hugging her.

	He's never coming back –
GINA	No, sweetheart, he'll come back. He'll come back, I promise. Nothing to cry about.
GREGORY	It's important to me that – it's important – Gina, look, do you believe that I only ever wanted the best for you?

GINA looks at GREGORY, as if she's seeing him for the first time.

GINA	You know, I do. But God help you.

GREGORY	Thank you. The best can still prevail. There's a happy ending here, Gina, I promise, it's going to be better than it's ever been –
HEDWIG	I'm never going to see him again –
GREGORY	Just a minute –
GINA	Don't you dare tell her to be quiet. Don't you dare.
	,
	Okay Heddy – I'm going after him – but you have to promise me you're going to stop these tears. Come on.
HEDWIG	Okay –
GINA	I'll be back.

She shouts down the stairs.

Francis! Francis! Hedwig, find your grandad –

GINA leaves. GREGORY sees the microphone, which has reappeared. He might be puzzled that it's reappeared.

GREGORY (m)	There's more to say. There's – there's – more to say –
	Ibsen. Ibsen – Ibsen fathered an illegitimate child on a serving girl. And the law forced him to pay for that child until the end of its thirteenth year – and thereafter, Ibsen had no contact *at all* with the child or its mother. And so *The Wild Duck* – *The Wild Duck* is his story is – a *lie* – a lie with something to prove, sold to audiences night after night after night – a lie that covers up what sort of father he *is*: and a lie that warns you to stay quiet, tells you that truth is destructive and corruption is better off *buried* – *The Wild Duck* is a lie.

HEDWIG   Why doesn't my daddy want to look at me
               any more?

GREGORY   It doesn't matter.

HEDWIG   It's because I'm not his child.

               ,

GREGORY   How could that be true?

   HEDWIG thinks.

HEDWIG   There was a story once where there was a
               baby left in the water in a basket in the reeds
               and they found it and kept it. Maybe I'm like
               that. Maybe Mummy found me and now
               Daddy's found out.

GREGORY   But –

HEDWIG   But even then, he could still love me. Maybe
               even love me *more*. I mean, the wild duck
               came to us by surprise and we're not its
               family but I still love it.

GREGORY   You love the wild duck. You really do –

HEDWIG   Yes

GREGORY   And it isn't yours. It is. But not in nature.

HEDWIG   I don't understand.

GREGORY   What *is* love?

HEDWIG   What do you mean?

GREGORY   How do you – show it?

HEDWIG   … you feel it, you don't show it.

GREGORY   So. It's a meaning kept under the surface.

   HEDWIG smiles

	We can make the world a better place if we trust our – our deepest sense of what is *right*. What is *true*. But those feelings get hidden, get buried –
HEDWIG	I didn't like it when he said he would hurt the wild duck. I say a prayer for her every single night. Because when she first came she was wounded, only now she's nearly healed, and I think that might be because she knows how much we love her.
GREGORY	So. What could you do to prove to your daddy how much you love him? There's nothing you wouldn't give up for him?
	,
	What's the thing you love most in the world? Apart from him and your mum.

HEDWIG points up to the loft. GREGORY nods.

HEDWIG	But he wanted to kill it.
GREGORY	He only wanted to end the lies. What if you sacrificed the wild duck?
HEDWIG	The wild duck?
GREGORY	If you gave up the thing that was most important to you –
	,
	to show to your dad what you feel?
HEDWIG	Kill it?
GREGORY	Sacrifice it.
HEDWIG	Why?

GREGORY	Because even if you're not his child, even if they found you in a basket, there's a deeper meaning: you still love your daddy as much as you possibly could, don't you?
HEDWIG	Yes
GREGORY	Even if you came from – the ends of the earth –
HEDWIG	from the deep of the green, salt sea.
	Do you think Daddy would understand it? That it had a meaning?
GREGORY	Yes.
HEDWIG	And love me even if I'm not / his child?
GREGORY	Yes.
HEDWIG	That would be beautiful –
GREGORY	Things are beautiful when we live honestly. I really believe that.
HEDWIG	Are you crying?
GREGORY	Am I [crying]?
HEDWIG	Would you like a hug? It's a sad night for everyone.

HEDWIG hugs GREGORY. A pause.

	I think I should ask Granddad to do it. Tomorrow morning.
GREGORY	Okay. But not a word to your mother.
HEDWIG	Why?
GREGORY	She doesn't understand us.

GINA comes back in.

GINA	He's not in the house, but they saw him with Relling.

GREGORY   He'll come back tonight. Don't worry. You'll
               see him before you go to bed. He'll come
               back.

GINA takes the microphone from GREGORY.

GINA (m)   He didn't come back.

*GREGORY and HEDWIG leave the stage. GINA stands there, aware
of the audience looking at her. Still on the microphone:*

               Please don't look at me like that.

               James didn't come home that night. He and
               Relling hit the bottle, withdrawing the little
               money left in his – in *our* current account,
               and drinking it. I think he slept at Relling's,
               I'm not sure.

               The next day – went by with no sign of him
               – until now. It's almost night.

               [ACT FIVE]

It's now the next day, HEDWIG's birthday. She starts to clear up the room.

               There is nothing. Blankness. There are a
               million things that you can *change,* later – to
               rebalance the negative, to alter the end result
               – temperature, time but really it comes down
               to two simple things: an exposure – and a
               blank sheet on which it will be written. A
               moment and its future impression. There
               is nothing at all. Blankness. And then as it
               blossoms into colour, as its shadows drop and
               its highlights hold firm – the image creeps into
               life. Out of the air, out of thin air, depth falls
               into a flat page – a cathedral, a hot air balloon,
               your sweetheart's face, his smile, his glass of
               drink, his head. Caught there forever. Held
               against time. This is what magic is. We are the
               writers of the eyes, and our ink is light

CHARLES	I'm / sorry
GINA	Oh my god I didn't see you there – I didn't see you –
CHARLES	Who were you talking to?

GINA is surprised – and then taken aback –

GINA	Myself. I didn't see you, I sometimes imagine – sorry, oh god it's stupid, really, I sometimes pretend I'm giving, like a lecture, a talk, the truth of [photography], if I'm having a bad day – it *doesn't matter*, sorry – *sorry* – what are you doing here?

GINA catches her breath, adjusts her appearance. She puts the microphone down.

CHARLES	I was looking for my son –
GINA	His room's downstairs.

,

CHARLES	Ah, sorry. To interrupt. It sounded / good
GINA	Please don't.
CHARLES	Are you having a bad day?
GINA	She said you'd gone away – your wife
CHARLES	I told her to say that. And she's not my wife.
GINA	Not *yet*.

There's a lot of conversation here, but very little in the lines.

CHARLES	No.

,

GINA	Your birthday present to Hedwig was incredibly generous.

CHARLES	Ah, yes?
	I try and give it away, try and share the luck.
	Look, you're not – we're not –
	Full disclosure: I actually came to see you.
	I feel I should say that I didn't want to, with everything going on these days, I don't want you to feel like you were in any way [abused] –
GINA	I don't feel that
CHARLES	Or that you were pressured –
GINA	I wasn't. I really wasn't, Charles
	I'm actually – it's actually – nice to see you. Again.
CHARLES	Ah – I'm glad –
GINA	I didn't ever mean to hurt you.
CHARLES	No, I know – you didn't *mean* to hurt anyone.
GINA	It doesn't mean I *didn't* hurt you, I realise that but –
CHARLES	No, I was heartbroken, actually – but it's a long time ago, now.
GINA	Doesn't *feel* it, though, does it? It sort of stands still in a strange way, like you can try and drive away from it, you can *drive*, if you want, but it's still on your windscreen. It's still there. Here. Sorry.
	God, I could never talk when you're around –
CHARLES	You could. You did.
GINA	Sometimes.
CHARLES	Sometimes – with your camera in your hand. Do you still have the one I / bought you?

GINA   Of course – yes, of course I do, that's the one
                        we use for the business, it's actually how we
                        make most of the money, two thirds of the
                        orders are people wanting photographic film,
                        for whatever reason – nostalgia, probably,
                        desperately wanting to pretend it's the past (!)

CHARLES   I can sympathise with that.

They smile.

                        Is she having a good birthday?

                        ,

*GINA opens her mouth. She lowers her head and then she speaks in
a way that really is honest.*

GINA   I think about you all the time. And there
                        are times when I don't know whether that
                        decision – whether it's him or [you]–

A whole other world becomes open and possible in this pause.

                        this is ridiculous, you need to turn round and
                        walk out of my home. Please.

CHARLES   Okay.

                        But do we need to talk? To have a
                        conversation?

GINA   No, we don't. We don't.

CHARLES   I see an old man in the mirror these days,
                        Gina, and in that respect alone I have no
                        doubt that you made the right decision for
                        yourself in all kinds of ways I don't or can't
                        or won't understand.

                        But from where I'm standing, I know this
                        much: I'll lie in the dark on my deathbed
                        and I'll think of the one mother and the
                        one father I had, and the one son – and I'll

wonder whether I also had one [true love] –
that is, whether a life with you, whether a life
with you – if there was *anything* I could have
done

That probably isn't true, is it? I don't think
I'll wonder at all. I can barely see now, but
on that bed, on that last day – I'll be seeing
your face

GREGORY appears at the door.

GREGORY   He won't see me, won't listen [to a word I say].

GREGORY sees CHARLES.

GINA   I'm going to change, you two can stay in
             here if you want –

GINA goes.

CHARLES   I've met a lot of people in my life, Gregory,
             and

GREGORY   I'm not *interested* in hearing your memoirs

             ,

CHARLES   and not one of those people thinks the way
             you do. I'm not sure what we did, what I
             did, that made you the way you are, I'm not
             even sure it's a bad thing, entirely, but – it's like:
             you're the protagonist of this construct called
             reality, and it's your job to force the rest of us to
             pull up our socks and sort the whole thing out.

             I can't say I'm proud of everything I did.
             Nobody can, I expect.

GREGORY   Right –

CHARLES   But I don't love to focus on the worst things
             in people. It doesn't give me any pleasure.
             I don't consider every person I meet to be

simply the worst part of themselves; I don't
think someone's failings always wipe out
their many thousand other things. And I
don't think true integrity is something you
have to perform.

RELLING appears.

Good evening, John.

And then to GREGORY:

I would appreciate it if you might give some
real thought to the company. I won't waste
your evening.

CHARLES goes.

RELLING   James is in the shower. Then he's coming up
             to get his things.

GREGORY   How is he?

RELLING   Hungover. You know how he grew up?

GREGORY   James? With his aunties, wasn't it –

RELLING   It was. The hero of the household. The best,
             most handsomest boy in the whole world.
             That's his problem.

GREGORY   He's an idealist, yes

RELLING   He's an idiot. And he's an idiot who's been
             told he's a genius.

GREGORY   That you think that reflects only on you.

RELLING   Enlighten me –

GREGORY   Because you're clearly disappointed with
             your life, you've forgotten who you were
             before – before you gave in. When you
             had hope that the broken old things would
             change – rather than just *shrug* and open a

bottle and put up with it – and all you can do is mock the people who could change things. Who will.

But there is a real truth, a purer human truth – which has become corralled, compromised and imprisoned and beaten down by corrupt people and corrupt systems and the weight of years of rotten history leaking down into it. And releasing it begins with telling the truth.

RELLING   And what's the collateral damage of that?

GREGORY   Truth is hard. People get hurt along the way. Like in any revolution.

RELLING   Truth is hard for James. A man incapable of surviving without the secret support of everyone around him – and whose ego would just crumble if he realised that was true –

GREGORY   I disagree.

RELLING   Because – on this subject – you're blind.

GREGORY   I think I see this situation pretty clearly –

RELLING   You're walking wounded. Carrying real damage. Here.

GREGORY   I know. I know.

,

RELLING   Always worshipping someone, fixated on some super-hero. Probably your dad, then when the scales fell from your eyes, your mum, and she's dead, she can't ruin the holy image, and now it's James Ekdal, and that's a bit beyond worship, but I bet there's been a few other innocents worshipped in between. Though he himself is the most pathetic.

GREGORY	If that's what you think of him, why live in his house?
RELLING	It's not.
GREGORY	What?
RELLING	He doesn't own this house. Your father does.

,

GREGORY	He bought their house?
RELLING	He did.
	And I live here because whatever you might think of me, I try and help him. Help them.
GREGORY	And what's your prescription? Whisky?
RELLING	The same one everyone else is on. The life lie.
GREGORY	The what?
RELLING	The life lie. It's a universal stimulant. The stories I tell them are the ones they tell themselves, and stories are *lies*. Even true stories. His dad didn't even need help: he self-medicates. The great military man, the noble hunter climbing up into the attic with a battered old handgun to chase around six rabbits, a handful of pigeons and an obese, domesticated duck.
GREGORY	I don't understand –
RELLING	He's *happy* – to him, those old Christmas trees held up with wires are towering forests, the pigeons are the wild game, sitting pert at the tops of the thousand-foot pines. It's a lie. But he's *happy*.
GREGORY	He's deluded

RELLING   So you'd – what? – tell him the truth? The
           thing you don't understand: is that telling the
           truth about things isn't the same as getting
           them to change.

           Pointing out the problem, getting angry about
           it, even, is not getting ideas to become real, *in
           the real world.* He's *happy.*

GREGORY   He's abandoned the ideals he had when he
           was young. / And that's *sad.*

RELLING   'Ideals' is a word from a foreign language.
           The word you're after is 'lies'.

GREGORY   They're not the same thing

RELLING   Oh, they really are. We hand out the same
           poison, me and you, only difference is the labels
           on the bottles. And my patients are happier.

GREGORY might be tearful.

GREGORY   That isn't what I'm doing – that isn't [what
           I'm doing] – if you want to talk about lies,
           my father, my *father* has – I was at school
           with James, and he was exceptional – a
           young *prince*, blessed with vision, he was
           going to *be someone who could do things* – and
           then my father flipped his dad onto his back,
           got to him, into him, wormed through the
           fabric of his life like a virus – he bought this
           house – he *bought* their fucking house

RELLING   I know

GREGORY   This carpet, this business, the photography
           studio, this piece of bread, the old man,
           Hedwig, every last thing you see has *him* in it
           like a virus – and he is *venom* –

RELLING   And you?

109

GREGORY	I'm nothing like him. I am nothing like him.
RELLING	People who don't feel liked tend to try to be right. Or make things right. Or sometimes pick up megaphones to scream their rightness at the world. But it's not rightness. Not really. It's pain.

,

GREGORY	I want James to break free from my father's lies. And I still believe he will.
RELLING	Then I feel sorry for him. Take away someone's life lie and you take their happiness with it. There's nothing left to live for.

HEDWIG comes in.

> Hey, mother of the wild duck, it's time for me to go and see where your daddy is.

RELLING goes out. GREGORY and HEDWIG look at each other.

GREGORY	I can tell you didn't do it.
HEDWIG	When I woke up it seemed like a strange idea. Not like it did yesterday.
GREGORY	You gave me real hope last night.
	Tell me. If the dog hadn't dived in, dived down, what would have happened to the duck?

FRANCIS comes in, coat on, wet –

FRANCIS	Not interrupting, I hope. It's horrible out there.
HEDWIG	Are you going hunting?

FRANCIS	It's cats and dogs. Bad hunting weather, my darling. Overcast. Can't hardly see your hand in front of your face.

GREGORY looks at HEDWIG and leaves.

HEDWIG	Grandad?
FRANCIS	Yes?
HEDWIG	Does it hurt the birds? Or the rabbits? Does it hurt the creatures who are hunted?
FRANCIS	What?
HEDWIG	The gun
FRANCIS	No, sweetheart – you stop their hearts. One bullet in the right place and they don't feel a thing. Like a light going out.
HEDWIG	Okay

GINA comes in.

FRANCIS	But we don't worry about that. I've got a present for you for dinnertime that you're going to absolutely love.
HEDWIG	Grandad –
FRANCIS	Yes –
HEDWIG	Why did you go to prison?
	,
FRANCIS	Because, my darling, I wasn't brave enough to do the right thing.

He kisses her on the head.

I'll get out of these wet things, smarten up –

He goes out.

GINA	Has he been for his walk?

As HEDWIG opens her mouth to answer, JAMES comes in, in a coat which is stained, badly, and perhaps ripped.

JAMES	I've come but I am going.
GINA	Yes – god, James, look at your coat.
JAMES	What?
GINA	Your good winter coat.
HEDWIG	Hello Daddy.
JAMES	Hello.

,

Could you go into your – Gina, could she go into the bedroom, please?

GINA	Give me a minute, Hedwig.

Tears in HEDWIG's eyes.

It seems for a moment as if HEDWIG isn't going to leave – but then, she does. GINA does too after a moment.

JAMES	I need my books. I'm going to need to take the books with me.

He opens – perhaps unlocks – drawers in the tables and takes out books and papers – that weren't there before. Real props now, to the very end.

The gun is taken out too.

I'm going to need them – for my invention, there's technical things – they're in there, actually in the cupboard, there's papers which –

GINA	They're here.

GINA has come back in with them. Suddenly the table seems full of things.

So you're really going to leave us?

,

JAMES	Do I have any choice?
	How can I *possibly* live like *this* – knowing what I know, everything I look / at reminding me –
GINA	Okay, I understand.
	What about Granddad?
JAMES	I know whose responsibility he is, Gina. My father will come with me.
GINA	Right.
JAMES	Are my glasses around here somewhere?
GINA	I – don't know. You had them / last night
JAMES	I had them last night but I can't find them this morning.
GINA	What did you *do* with them, James?
JAMES	It's not really your concern, is it?

GINA goes out. JAMES bangs around drawers, looking for things.

Fucking Relling. Someone should push him down the bloody stairs.

The two halves of the letter he tore up stare back at him from the table. He looks at them. He picks them up. Then GINA comes back in, with a tray. He puts them down, fast.

GINA There's a coffee there for you. And there's bread and butter and some other bits and pieces.

| JAMES | I can't eat here, Gina. I haven't eaten for – since yesterday – but it doesn't matter, I just need to get my things and get out. |
| | |

I'm missing a notebook – which I left in …

He opens the door and HEDWIG is right behind it –

Oh GOD everywhere I LOOK.

He doesn't mean to be cruel, the frustration is from real pain and sadness –

GINA	She has to be somewhere.
JAMES	Can you *please* go into your *bedroom* –
HEDWIG	I'm sorry daddy – I'm really sorry for everything.
JAMES *(at once)*	Gina, can you please get her to –
GINA *(at once)*	It's not your fault, sweetheart, there's nothing to be sorry for
HEDWIG	*Please* don't go away from us –

JAMES goes off into the kitchen, away from her.

GINA	Please, Hedwig, give us a minute. Go downstairs.

GINA follows him out.

HEDWIG, alone on stage. She looks at what's on the table. Her eyes are hurting. She picks up the gun from the table and exits as, from off, we hear the below: as the door re-opens and JAMES re-enters with a bag, mid-conversation.

| JAMES | That bag will in no way be big enough to take everything I have to take, and we do have a bigger one, I swear we have a – we had a – |

JAMES slumps in a chair –

I'm finding this hard and exhausting to have to pack, while –

He gestures to where HEDWIG was. He puts his head in his hands.

,

GINA   Take a shirt and some underwear and get the rest later. Your coffee's getting cold.

He takes a sip of his coffee.

                     I don't know if you've thought about – the animals – if you're going to take them too.

JAMES   How can I take them?

GINA   I don't know how Granddad will feel without / them

JAMES   He'll have to learn. There won't be the space, with what I can afford, for him to have his forest – I'm having to give up more than that, so he –

JAMES thinks about how much he's going to have to lose if he leaves. His resolve slightly slackens.

GINA   Do you want to take the record player?

JAMES   Yes. No. No record player. But I should [take the gun] – where's the gun?

GINA   It was sitting there. He must have taken it up with him.

JAMES   Is he up in the attic?

GINA   Where else would he be?

Tiny smile – tiny thawing – he's looking at the bread and butter.

JAMES   It's sleet and rain out there.

He takes a piece of bread. He's looking for something on the table.

GINA   What are you looking for?

JAMES   Butter?

GINA   Coming up

JAMES   No, you don't have to – it doesn't matter –

She gives him the butter, in the butter dish. He butters his bread. A sense of completion here, a sense that some part of the final picture is clear.

GINA   James. Is this the end?

,

I mean, are we going to – get divorced?

Is this it?

,

JAMES   I don't know. I don't know what I feel. I don't know what you feel.

GINA   It doesn't feel like the end. And I don't – I don't want not to be there for when you're ill and when you're old and when your invention is finished. I don't want Hedwig to have two sets of presents at Christmas. I don't want that life for her when she could have this one – has had –

I have been so scared of this. I don't *know* if I love you. I don't – but it's my best guess that I do because I don't know what other people mean when they say those words. I don't know if I match up. I have this fear, that really the whole time I've understood something completely different, and one day they'll look into my head and be like – *what? No.* And say, no, your whole life was like an optical conclusion.

A crack in his armour – this is funny – he can't let it go by, somehow –

JAMES   Illusion. Optical illusion.

GINA   I'm sorry, yes. I mean: to be in love. In
                        love. Inside love. It's the world you live in,
                        not a thing that happens to you.

                        I know that this is reaping what I sowed – I
                        do know that, I know I had this coming to
                        me, but I don't know, Jamesy, I do wonder
                        if this is the thing that's going to bring us
                        closer together and give us a new start, and
                        if stupid crazy Gregers might actually have
                        had a point and it might – maybe it – now
                        the worst has happened and we're still here,
                        we're still alive and we still love each other.
                        I hope.

                        ,

                        But if you can listen to this music and look
                        me in the face in this room, in this little nest
                        at the top of the house, that we made, away
                        from the noise, and the world, then – then
                        then really this is the end of the story

JAMES   Gina –

*She puts a record on. It hisses for a while, and then a song plays.
FRANCIS enters, talking into the microphone.*

FRANCIS (m)   The record player was bought some years
                        earlier at an auction and had been sold to
                        James as a rarity: an art deco turntable and
                        matching speakers made by Decca in 1969.
                        That the Decca logo didn't appear on it
                        anywhere suggested that in fact its history
                        might be a fiction. But that's so often the
                        way it goes.

*The introduction plays. JAMES holds out his hands to GINA, like
a baby. She lifts him into her arms, and JAMES sobs into GINA's
shoulder. She strokes his hair and comforts him. She tells him, again
and again, that she's sorry. The two of them start to dance. They're*

a bit silly with each other, both trying to stop his tears. She holds his face and says again that she's sorry. He says he's sorry too.

I don't know where they first heard it – but this song was the kids' choice for the first dance at their wedding reception: and as it played, as evening fell, twenty tables, entangled in strings of lights, one by one, went dark, until the couple, wound together, wrapped in lines of light, were the only thing visible – dancing, alone against the darkcloth of the night.

The couple dance.

Of course, I missed the wedding. And now, tonight, I didn't even remember that story – but when, sitting in my bedroom, I heard that song, the rootless, unpindownable feeling of happiness it triggered flowed through my body like rain.

I didn't know that, only two weeks later, a blood vessel would explode in my head as I was slowly ascending the stairs from the bathroom, and that my body would lie there until morning before it was found.

You see, I hadn't opened the letter, my results, because I didn't want to know. Or because somewhere I did know, and I didn't want to see. But we're all just walking, ticking time bombs, aren't we? Who needs the truth?

The music plays. HEDWIG enters. She sees her parents dancing together. They don't see her.

The loft is revealed, exactly as we have imagined it. It completes the picture of the Ekdal family home. HEDWIG looks up at the loft.

She smiles. She climbs the ladder and disappears into its darkness.

The song finishes, or maybe the song skips. It shouldn't end. The turntable hisses.

JAMES   I don't know

                   I know it's –

                   I don't know.

GINA   You don't know what?

JAMES   I don't know what this means, now.

                   I don't know what happens next.

                   I don't really know who you *are* any more.

GREGORY comes in.

GREGORY   Should I go?

GINA   You're a part of what's happened. As much
                   as anyone. I'm telling James that we can start
                   again. You can work on your / invention –

JAMES   Oh *come on* that's not a real thing.

                          ,

                   Relling started me off on it, it made me
                   happy to think I might actually achieve
                   something – but it was when Hedwig started
                   to believe in it, I mean, I let myself think that
                   she did –

                   I loved that child. It was the greatest part of
                   my day every day to come back to this house
                   and see her little face and now I don't know
                   any more. I don't know.

GREGORY   You don't know what?

                          ,

JAMES   Did she ever love me?

119

GREGORY	You can't be seriously doubting *that*
JAMES	I am. Because if she isn't mine, and it's – the eyes, you know, it's *likely* she isn't mine
GINA	She's yours in every way that matters
JAMES	Then why this letter?

He picks up the two halves of the letter.

Her father's calling to her. Anna loves her, you know that, they'd love to have her. And here it is, handsfull of gold and they're offering her a life

| GINA | And what do you think she'll say? |

Commotion in the loft – rustling, the duck quacks.

| JAMES | She's not old enough to know yet. She'd have to be an adult. Have to understand what was being offered. Because she would have to give up a whole *life*. Her life, which is hers by rights, hers by birth, she would have to give it up – and why would she? Why would she want to stay – for a man who isn't her father, isn't her blood, with no money, no education, in a rented flat with her alcoholic grandad? Why would she give up her life for some dead-dog photographer lounging around useless with nowhere to go? |

A real pistol shot is heard from the attic. It's loud.

GINA	What's he doing, hunting on his own? I thought we said –
GREGORY	You don't know what that means
GINA	Sorry?

GREGORY   She did it. He did it, but she asked him to –
            he's shot the wild duck.

                ,

JAMES   Shot the wild duck?

GINA   Why?

GREGORY   She wanted to sacrifice the thing that was
            most precious to her in the world. For you.
            She wanted you to love her again.

*JAMES is moved – this feels like it could be a happy ending – GINA
also tearful.*

JAMES   Hedwig?

GREGORY   Yes

JAMES   Oh little Hedwig –

GINA   You see, James? You see?

GREGORY smiles, moved too –

GREGORY   She wanted her dad. She couldn't live
            without him.

JAMES   Where is she?

The fire alarm starts.

GINA   She's in her bedroom –

JAMES   Hedwig – HEDWIG!

He runs into her bedroom. No HEDWIG –

            is she in the kitchen?

GINA moves to check –

GINA   Heddy?

FRANCIS appears in his military uniform, green jacket and all.

FRANCIS   Where is she?

JAMES   I thought you were up there?

FRANCIS   Are we ready?

He's got a birthday cake for HEDWIG, in the shape of a duck.

GINA   Did you fire the gun?

FRANCIS   When?

GINA   Now – just now

JAMES has instinctively climbed the ladder, fast. Perhaps he switches on a light which reveals the loft as less magical than we thought – more real. Or if you like, more fake.

FRANCIS   Me?

GREGORY   She's killed the wild duck.

JAMES has found HEDWIG

JAMES   Hedwig? What are you doing down there?

Sudden desperation sets in –

                 Help – *help* – the gun's warm – oh god, she's
                 on the floor – Gregers, help me, help me get
                 her down

JAMES, in the loft, picks up HEDWIG and he and GREGORY get HEDWIG down out of the loft, as GINA runs to the door and screams out of it.

GINA   Relling – Relling – call an ambulance – call
                 an ambulance – it's the gun, it's HEDDY,
                 it's the gun – oh god, be gentle with her –
                 careful, careful, Hedwig, it's your mum, I'm
                 here, sweetheart, I'm right here –

FRANCIS   The forest has had its revenge.

JAMES sends the contents of the table – butter, bread, the lot – flying to make room for HEDWIG's little body.

GINA   We can't put her on a hard table – she's
                bleeding – oh god, she's bleeding –

*Blood everywhere. GREGORY's trying to blanche the wound with
white kitchen roll and blood is getting all over it.*

JAMES   She's coming round – she's going to come
                round –

GINA   Get out of the way – get out of the way I
                can't find where she's / shot herself –

JAMES   It isn't serious, Gina, it's not a serious thing,
                she's going to be all right, she's going to be
                all right – she's going to be all right –

*RELLING enters on the phone, adrenalin pulsing through his body
– he's visible, slurringly, embarrassingly drunk.*

*GREGORY and JAMES may well need to ad lib a bit – but there
shouldn't be silence until the realisation starts to drop.*

RELLING   It's a bullet wound –

GINA   HELP HER

JAMES   Hedwig, Hedwig, you have to keep
                breathing, we have to keep breathing,
                Hedwig – / we're all here with you Hedwig,
                we're all here, can you see us, Heddy, can
                you see any of us, any sign you can give us –

RELLING   How old is she? Gina, how old is she?

GINA   She's thirteen – for fuck's sake hurry – she
                isn't breathing –

RELLING   Thirteen – yes / yes – sorry, someone is on
                their way?

*Maybe RELLING opens a first-aid kit, drunkenly and the contents
go everywhere.*

GINA   She isn't breathing – she isn't breathing –

RELLING   I don't think she's conscious, no –

RELLING tries to find a pulse –

JAMES   And scene – and *scene* –

                 HEDWIG STOP THIS AND STAND UP, this isn't
                 funny – oh god, Hedwig, this isn't funny –
                 and *SCENE –*

                          ,

Nothing happens.

RELLING   I do apologise, I'm a little drunk so it night
                 might have been, be difficult – could you
                 send somebody *immediately*?

GINA grabs the phone from RELLING

GINA   It's her mum – no, no – no no she's not, she's
                 not – she's not – she's not –

*As FRANCIS moves to GINA, the truth is in his eyes. GINA drops the
phone and slumps into FRANCIS' arms. And then, primal, maternal,
screams and batters a cushion and feathers go everywhere. It looks
as if a duck has died. And bled. Ducks bleed. After that storm
exhausts itself, she says to JAMES.*

                 She's yours now, as much as mine.

JAMES   Take her downstairs – for when they get here –

*As JAMES carries her out, RELLING opening the door for him,
GINA helps him lift the body. Only GREGORY and RELLING left.
Stunned. RELLING hands the microphone to GREGERS.*

GREGORY (m)   Hedwig Ekdal committed suicide on her
                 thirteenth birthday. But for James and Gina
                 Ekdal, it was a new beginning. They were
                 changed. James Ekdal was a different man.

RELLING (m)   For a year. Most people feel noble in the
                 presence of death. And then: it fades.

GREGORY (m)   The truth is –

              The truth of the story

              It can't be that this *justifies* his his

RELLING (m)   A year later the memory of Hedwig Ekdal
              became just another self-aggrandising, self-
              pitying anecdote. With what had happened,
              James Ekdal crafted a story to suit him –
              because reality was simply too painful.

GREGORY   If you're right about that, then – if that's what
              this means, then

              why do any of us stay alive?

                   ,

RELLING looks at GREGERS.

RELLING (m)   Gregory Woods hanged himself. Good
              riddance.

GREGORY (m)   But something

              something of what he stood for survived. It is
              with us. It lives on.

With real contempt, RELLING shakes his head – and laughs.

And spits on the floor at GREGORY's feet.

And then goes out of the front door, perhaps laughing.

GREGORY stands in the middle of the stage, just as at the beginning.

He clicks the mic on.

Clicks it off.

He looks like he's about to say something. Draws breath.

And then the rest of the cast enter to join him for the curtain call.

ALMEIDA
THEATRE

The Almeida Theatre makes brave new work that asks big questions: of plays, of theatre and of the world around us.

Whether new work or reinvigorated classics, the Almeida brings together the most exciting artists to take risks; to provoke, inspire and surprise our audiences.

Recent highlights include Rupert Goold's Olivier Award-winning production of *Ink* (transferred to the West End and transfers to Broadway in 2019), Robert Icke's productions of *Hamlet* (transferred to the West End and was broadcast on BBC TWO) and *Mary Stuart* (transferred to the West End and toured the UK) and Rebecca Frecknall's production of *Summer and Smoke* (which transfers to the West End in November 2018).

Other notable productions have included *American Psycho: a new musical thriller* (transferred to Broadway); *Chimerica* (won three Olivier Awards and transferred to the West End); *King Charles III* (won the Olivier Award for Best New Play and transferred to the West End and Broadway, toured the UK and Sydney, and was adapted into a BAFTA nominated TV drama); and *Oresteia* (transferred to the West End and won the Olivier Award for Best Director).

Andrew Scott in *Hamlet*, directed by Robert Icke at the Almeida Theatre (2017). Photo by Manuel Harlan.

Artistic Director **Rupert Goold**

Executive Director **Denise Wood**

Associate Directors **Robert Icke, Rebecca Frecknall**

almeida.co.uk
🐦 @AlmeidaTheatre
📘 /almeidatheatre
📷 @almeida_theatre

Supported using public funding by
ARTS COUNCIL ENGLAND

Registered charity number 282167

LONDON THEATRE OF THE YEAR 2018
THE STAGE AWARDS

Principal Partner

ASPEN